THE EPISTLE OF ST JAMES
AND
JUDAIC CHRISTIANITY

T0382303

THE EPISTLE OF ST JAMES
AND
JUDAIC CHRISTIANITY

BY

GERALD H. RENDALL, B.D., LITT.D., LL.D.

Fellow of Trinity College, Cambridge 1875–1882; Principal
of Liverpool University 1880–1897; Head Master
of Charterhouse 1897–1911; Examining
Chaplain and Hon. Canon
of Chelmsford

CAMBRIDGE

AT THE UNIVERSITY PRESS

1927

CAMBRIDGE
UNIVERSITY PRESS

University Printing House, Cambridge CB2 8BS, United Kingdom

Cambridge University Press is part of the University of Cambridge.

It furthers the University's mission by disseminating knowledge in the pursuit of education, learning and research at the highest international levels of excellence.

www.cambridge.org
Information on this title: www.cambridge.org/9781107440609

© Cambridge University Press 1927

First published 1927
First paperback edition 2014

A catalogue record for this publication is available from the British Library

ISBN 978-1-107-44060-9 Paperback

ἡ στήλη μένει παρὰ τῷ ναῷ·
ΜΑΡΤΥϹ ΟΥΤΟϹ ΑΛΗΘΗϹ
ΙΟΥΔΑΙΟΙϹ ΤΕ ΚΑΙ ΕΛΛΗϹΙΝ.

HEGESIPPUS, ap. *Euseb. H. E.* ii. 23

CONTENTS

Introductory . . . . *page* 1

Επιστολη Ιακωβου 5

Chapter I. The Superscription 11

II. Personality, Career and Surroundings . . 16

III. James and his Readers 25

IV. Form, Style and Composition . . . 34

V. Ethic 42

VI. Doctrine 61

VII. Faith and Works 71

VIII. Christology 88

IX. Relation to other Books—Canonical and Sub-
Apostolic 96

X. Late Authorship and Date 103

XI. The Church at Jerusalem, under the Leadership of James 110

XII. Values of the Epistle 118

XIII. Epilogue—Clementine *Recognitions* and *Homilies* 133

Index 141

Index of N.T. Texts 145

INTRODUCTORY

By the end of last century Textual Criticism of the Greek Testament had virtually completed its task: refinements and intricacies remained as the hunting-ground of specialists, but the foundations of a trustworthy text were securely laid, and interest passed decisively into the wider and more complex problems of the Higher Criticism, whose task it is to co-ordinate the various data—documentary, historical and religious—into an organic whole. The collection and sorting of materials may now be regarded as complete; it is little likely that much, if anything, of crucial importance will be added to the existing finds: they have been scrutinised and analysed, and subjected to the many-sided tests of the philologist, the exegete, the theologian and the historian. And the results at first blush look more like a chaos of conflicting and irreconcileable hypotheses than a body of ascertained and reasoned truth. But the Higher Criticism is not destined to end in self-confusion: each specialist has had his say, often approaching his subject with one-sided prepossessions, or in the interests of foregone conclusions: but the problems submitted are not insoluble, and sooner or later the exaggerations or vagaries of specialists are brought to book, and reduced to proportion and to unity.

The Higher Criticism of the Homeric Poems may serve as an example and encouragement; for a full century from the publication of Wolf's *Prolegomena* in 1795, the whole trend of criticism seemed destructive. Ballad and Lay and Saga theories of composition, Sun Myth and Nature Myth, all had their day: the separatist and the disintegrator careered at large. Not only literary unity, but the very possibility of literary transmission was scornfully denied. Historic truth or validity was a mere backwater of the pedant and the die-hard: scarped Ilium or Mycenæ rich-in-gold, long-haired Achæans or horse-taming Trojans, were but figments of late poetic fancy. But to-day, as the final outcome of piecemeal analysis and microscopic erudition, the successive phases of Ægean and Minoan civilisation, the place of Mycenæan culture, and of Achæan dominance in their development, the *raison d'être* of the leaguer of Ilium, the relation of the Homeric poems to these episodes in Ægean history, have gained their accepted place in the scheme of Mediterranean development, and become in turn trustworthy criteria for further determinations and research. In the field of New Testament study, one cannot indeed hope for revelations as dramatic and decisive as those which at Hissarlik, Mycenæ and Knossos the spade and the archæologist have contributed to Ægean history, but bit by bit exploration and topography, the papyri and epigraphy, are directing new rays of light upon the doings and the ways of thought in the Church of the first days: from time to time some document of first-rate importance is brought to light; and the more intensive sifting of known sources proves by no means barren of results. As an illustration in our chosen field, among English writers, the contributions of Charles, Fairweather, Thackeray, Lightley and others, and not less the searchlights turned upon the Synoptic records by Jewish experts and Hebraists such as Montefiore, Friedländer, Abrahams and Klausner, are invaluable for correct orientation of the Epistle of James, for appreciation of the lie of parties and principles, the atmosphere and the conditions under which the Epistle came into being.

Confusion still abounds. Just as in departments of theology, whole schemes of doctrine and discipline have been erected upon single texts or phrases torn from their literary context or their historic *milieu*, so too in Higher Criticism detached and isolated phrases, chance correspondences or even innocent omissions have been made the basis for specious but flimsy generalisations—scenic but unsubstantial—which cannot bear the impact of fuller data and more organic research. Meanwhile they cumber the ground and discredit the implements employed in their production. But over against them the sum of constructive results accumulates: *Tekel* has been written on not a few pretentious fabrics; hypotheses that once seemed plausible are passing to the limbo of the obsolete. 'Truth lies in the accord of all the constituent factors.'[1] Not only in respect of the Pauline Epistles, but likewise of the Synoptists, and even of Johannine literature, the margins of variation are steadily decreasing, both in time and place. The products of Judaic Christianity stand in somewhat different case: the total output is small, the secular contacts much more restricted, and the documentary data for comparison scanty. A characteristic of Jewish thought—as evinced in the whole mass of Rabbinic literature—is a pervading stationariness and concentration of interest, that seems impervious to lapse of time, to change of surrounding and to the passage of events. Such factors militate against precise determinations of date or provenance. Yet the materials in my belief suffice to prove that the Epistle of James belongs to the middle of the first century[2], and the object of the present study is to gain a clear idea of its own values, and its relation to other books, canonical and extra-canonical.

For just appraisement of Western, or of Alexandrine Christianity, right understanding of Judaic—its aims and its destinies— is essential. As in a puzzle, each piece fitted into its place assists the setting of the companion pieces and the effect of the *ensemble*. I have not aimed at detailed, still less complete, exegesis of the Epistle in all its parts. That ground has been covered by Mayor, by Spitta, by Zahn, by Hort, and by other exegetes among whom English commentators hold so commanding a place. Nor have I attempted any complete investigation of doctrine. Rather, my aim has been to concentrate on all points that bear on authorship and provenance and date, and to gather up the synthesis that results from the combined labours of students, with whose learning, range and industry my own cannot compare. I have not loaded my pages with references, but anyone who knows the ground will recognise that I have studied carefully the work of previous expositors. Full bibliographies will be found in Mayor *Ep. St James* and in Moffatt *Introduction to Lit. N. T.* Among later English expositions I may add R. St J. Parry *Discussion of Gen. Ep. of St James* (1903), Boyd Carpenter *Wisdom of James the Just* (1903), W. Patrick *James the Lord's Brother* (1906),

---

[1] τῷ ἀληθεῖ πάντα συνᾴδει τὰ ὑπάρχοντα Arist. *Nic. Eth.* i. 8.
[2] Cf. Knox *St Paul and the Church of Jerusalem* p. 21.

Hort *Ep. St James* (1909), H. Maynard Smith *Ep. St James* (1914), Ropes in *Internat. Crit. Comm.* (1916), among whom in linguistic exegesis Hort stands supreme. For the better understanding of Judaic Christianity, Montefiore in *Synoptic Gospels*, *Bible for Home Reading*, *Old Test. and After*, Abrahams in *Studies of Pharisaism* I and II and smaller works, Klausner *Jesus of Nazareth*, supply invaluable helps, and on the historical side the recent volumes of Lightley on *Jewish Sects and Parties in the Time of Christ*, W. L. Knox *St Paul and the Church of Jerusalem*, abound in interest.

The Epistle does not occupy much space; and for convenience of reference I have reprinted, with the permission of the publishers, Messrs Macmillan and Co. Ltd, the Greek text as edited by Westcott and Hort[1]. The uncials are a useful index to O.T. references, though they by no means exhaust that field of observation. But throughout I have borne in mind the English reader, and except in Chap. IV, devoted to diction and vocabulary, Chap. VII Appendix, and Chap. IX, which deals with parallel books, have so far as possible restricted Greek to brackets, Notes, or Appendices.

[1] At the end of v. 6 I omit the interrogation, which Ropes stands almost alone in approving. Reasons are given on p. 94.

ΙΑΚΩΒΟΥ ΕΠΙΣΤΟΛΗ

Ἰάκωβος θεοῦ καὶ κυρίου Ἰησοῦ Χριστοῦ δοῦλος ταῖς 1 δώδεκα φυλαῖς ταῖς ἐν τῇ διασπορᾷ χαίρειν.

Πᾶσαν χαρὰν ἡγήσασθε, ἀδελφοί μου, ὅταν πειρασμοῖς 2 περιπέσητε ποικίλοις, γινώσκοντες ὅτι τὸ δοκίμιον ὑμῶν τῆς 3 πίστεως κατεργάζεται ὑπομονήν· ἡ δὲ ὑπομονὴ ἔργον τέλειον 4 ἐχέτω, ἵνα ἦτε τέλειοι καὶ ὁλόκληροι, ἐν μηδενὶ λειπόμενοι. Εἰ δέ τις ὑμῶν λείπεται σοφίας, αἰτείτω παρὰ τοῦ διδόντος 5 θεοῦ πᾶσιν ἁπλῶς καὶ μὴ ὀνειδίζοντος, καὶ δοθήσεται αὐτῷ· αἰτείτω δὲ ἐν πίστει, μηδὲν διακρινόμενος, ὁ γὰρ διακρινόμενος 6 ἔοικεν κλύδωνι θαλάσσης ἀνεμιζομένῳ καὶ ῥιπιζομένῳ· μὴ 7 γὰρ οἰέσθω ὁ ἄνθρωπος ἐκεῖνος ὅτι λήμψεταί τι παρὰ τοῦ κυρίου ἀνὴρ δίψυχος, ἀκατάστατος ἐν πάσαις ταῖς ὁδοῖς 8 αὐτοῦ. Καυχάσθω δὲ [ὁ] ἀδελφὸς ὁ ταπεινὸς ἐν τῷ ὕψει αὐτοῦ, 9 ὁ δὲ πλούσιος ἐν τῇ ταπεινώσει αὐτοῦ, ὅτι ὡς ἄνθος χόρτου 10 παρελεύσεται. ἀνέτειλεν γὰρ ὁ ἥλιος σὺν τῷ καύσωνι καὶ 11 ἐξήρανεν τὸν χόρτον, καὶ τὸ ἄνθος αὐτοῦ ἐξέπεσεν καὶ ἡ εὐπρέπεια τοῦ προσώπου αὐτοῦ ἀπώλετο· οὕτως καὶ ὁ πλούσιος ἐν ταῖς πορείαις αὐτοῦ μαρανθήσεται. Μακάριος ἀνὴρ ὃς 12 ὑπομένει πειρασμόν, ὅτι δόκιμος γενόμενος λήμψεται τὸν στέφανον τῆς ζωῆς, ὃν ἐπηγγείλατο τοῖς ἀγαπῶσιν αὐτόν. μηδεὶς πειραζόμενος λεγέτω ὅτι Ἀπὸ θεοῦ πειράζομαι· ὁ γὰρ 13 θεὸς ἀπείραστός ἐστιν κακῶν, πειράζει δὲ αὐτὸς οὐδένα. ἕκασ- 14 τος δὲ πειράζεται ὑπὸ τῆς ἰδίας ἐπιθυμίας ἐξελκόμενος καὶ δελεαζόμενος· εἶτα ἡ ἐπιθυμία συλλαβοῦσα τίκτει ἁμαρτίαν, 15 ἡ δὲ ἁμαρτία ἀποτελεσθεῖσα ἀποκυεῖ θάνατον. Μὴ πλανᾶσθε, 16 ἀδελφοί μου ἀγαπητοί. πᾶσα δόσις ἀγαθὴ καὶ πᾶν δώρημα 17 τέλειον ἄνωθέν ἐστιν, καταβαῖνον ἀπὸ τοῦ πατρὸς τῶν φώτων, παρ' ᾧ οὐκ ἔνι παραλλαγὴ ἢ τροπῆς ἀποσκίασμα. βουληθεὶς 18 ἀπεκύησεν ἡμᾶς λόγῳ ἀληθείας, εἰς τὸ εἶναι ἡμᾶς ἀπαρχήν τινα τῶν αὐτοῦ κτισμάτων.

Ἴστε, ἀδελφοί μου ἀγαπητοί. ἔστω δὲ πᾶς ἄνθρωπος ταχὺς 19

20 εἰς τὸ ἀκοῦσαι, βραδὺς εἰς τὸ λαλῆσαι, βραδὺς εἰς ὀργήν, ὀργὴ
21 γὰρ ἀνδρὸς δικαιοσύνην θεοῦ οὐκ ἐργάζεται. διὸ ἀποθέμενοι
πᾶσαν ῥυπαρίαν καὶ περισσείαν κακίας ἐν πραΰτητι δέξασθε
τὸν ἔμφυτον λόγον τὸν δυνάμενον σῶσαι τὰς ψυχὰς ὑμῶν.
22 Γίνεσθε δὲ ποιηταὶ λόγου καὶ μὴ ἀκροαταὶ μόνον παραλογι-
23 ζόμενοι ἑαυτούς. ὅτι εἴ τις ἀκροατὴς λόγου ἐστὶν καὶ οὐ
ποιητής, οὗτος ἔοικεν ἀνδρὶ κατανοοῦντι τὸ πρόσωπον τῆς
24 γενέσεως αὐτοῦ ἐν ἐσόπτρῳ, κατενόησεν γὰρ ἑαυτὸν καὶ
25 ἀπελήλυθεν καὶ εὐθέως ἐπελάθετο ὁποῖος ἦν. ὁ δὲ παρακύψας
εἰς νόμον τέλειον τὸν τῆς ἐλευθερίας καὶ παραμείνας, οὐκ
ἀκροατὴς ἐπιλησμονῆς γενόμενος ἀλλὰ ποιητὴς ἔργου, οὗτος
26 μακάριος ἐν τῇ ποιήσει αὐτοῦ ἔσται. Εἴ τις δοκεῖ θρησκὸς
εἶναι μὴ χαλιναγωγῶν γλῶσσαν ἑαυτοῦ ἀλλὰ ἀπατῶν καρδίαν
27 ἑαυτοῦ, τούτου μάταιος ἡ θρησκεία. θρησκεία καθαρὰ καὶ
ἀμίαντος παρὰ τῷ θεῷ καὶ πατρὶ αὕτη ἐστίν, ἐπισκέπτεσθαι
ὀρφανοὺς καὶ χήρας ἐν τῇ θλίψει αὐτῶν, ἄσπιλον ἑαυτὸν
τηρεῖν ἀπὸ τοῦ κόσμου.

II Ἀδελφοί μου, μὴ ἐν προσωπολημψίαις ἔχετε τὴν πίστιν
2 τοῦ κυρίου ἡμῶν Ἰησοῦ Χριστοῦ τῆς δόξης; ἐὰν γὰρ εἰσέλθῃ
εἰς συναγωγὴν ὑμῶν ἀνὴρ χρυσοδακτύλιος ἐν ἐσθῆτι λαμπρᾷ,
3 εἰσέλθῃ δὲ καὶ πτωχὸς ἐν ῥυπαρᾷ ἐσθῆτι, ἐπιβλέψητε δὲ ἐπὶ
τὸν φοροῦντα τὴν ἐσθῆτα τὴν λαμπρὰν καὶ εἴπητε Σὺ κάθου
ὧδε καλῶς, καὶ τῷ πτωχῷ εἴπητε Σὺ στῆθι ἢ κάθου ἐκεῖ ὑπὸ
4 τὸ ὑποπόδιόν μου, οὐ διεκρίθητε ἐν ἑαυτοῖς καὶ ἐγένεσθε
5 κριταὶ διαλογισμῶν πονηρῶν; Ἀκούσατε, ἀδελφοί μου
ἀγαπητοί. οὐχ ὁ θεὸς ἐξελέξατο τοὺς πτωχοὺς τῷ κόσμῳ
πλουσίους ἐν πίστει καὶ κληρονόμους τῆς βασιλείας ἧς
6 ἐπηγγείλατο τοῖς ἀγαπῶσιν αὐτόν; ὑμεῖς δὲ ἠτιμάσατε τὸν
πτωχόν. οὐχ οἱ πλούσιοι καταδυναστεύουσιν ὑμῶν, καὶ αὐτοὶ
7 ἕλκουσιν ὑμᾶς εἰς κριτήρια; οὐκ αὐτοὶ βλασφημοῦσιν τὸ
8 καλὸν ὄνομα τὸ ἐπικληθὲν ἐφ᾽ ὑμᾶς; εἰ μέντοι νόμον τελεῖτε
βασιλικὸν κατὰ τὴν γραφήν ΑΓΑΠΗCΕΙC ΤΟΝ ΠΛΗCΙΟΝ CΟΥ ὡς
9 CΕΑΥΤΟΝ, καλῶς ποιεῖτε· εἰ δὲ προσωπολημπτεῖτε, ἁμαρτίαν
10 ἐργάζεσθε, ἐλεγχόμενοι ὑπὸ τοῦ νόμου ὡς παραβάται. Ὅστις

γὰρ ὅλον τὸν νόμον τηρήσῃ, πταίσῃ δὲ ἐν ἑνί, γέγονεν πάντων
ἔνοχος. ὁ γὰρ εἰπών Μὴ μοιχεύςῃς εἶπεν καί Μὴ φονεύςῃς· 11
εἰ δὲ οὐ μοιχεύεις φονεύεις δέ, γέγονας παραβάτης νόμου.
οὕτως λαλεῖτε καὶ οὕτως ποιεῖτε ὡς διὰ νόμου ἐλευθερίας 12
μέλλοντες κρίνεσθαι. ἡ γὰρ κρίσις ἀνέλεος τῷ μὴ ποιήσαντι 13
ἔλεος· κατακαυχᾶται ἔλεος κρίσεως.   Τί ὄφελος, ἀδελ- 14
φοί μου, ἐὰν πίστιν λέγῃ τις ἔχειν ἔργα δὲ μὴ ἔχῃ; μὴ δύναται
ἡ πίστις σῶσαι αὐτόν; ἐὰν ἀδελφὸς ἢ ἀδελφὴ γυμνοὶ ὑπάρ- 15
χωσιν καὶ λειπόμενοι τῆς ἐφημέρου τροφῆς, εἴπῃ δέ τις αὐτοῖς 16
ἐξ ὑμῶν Ὑπάγετε ἐν εἰρήνῃ, θερμαίνεσθε καὶ χορτάζεσθε, μὴ
δῶτε δὲ αὐτοῖς τὰ ἐπιτήδεια τοῦ σώματος, τί ὄφελος; οὕτως 17
καὶ ἡ πίστις, ἐὰν μὴ ἔχῃ ἔργα, νεκρά ἐστιν καθ' ἑαυτήν.
ἀλλ' ἐρεῖ τις Σὺ πίστιν ἔχεις κἀγὼ ἔργα ἔχω. δεῖξον μοι τὴν 18
πίστιν σου χωρὶς τῶν ἔργων, κἀγώ σοι δείξω ἐκ τῶν ἔργων
μου τὴν πίστιν. σὺ πιστεύεις ὅτι εἷς θεὸς ἔστιν; καλῶς 19
ποιεῖς· καὶ τὰ δαιμόνια πιστεύουσιν καὶ φρίσσουσιν. θέλεις 20
δὲ γνῶναι, ὦ ἄνθρωπε κενέ, ὅτι ἡ πίστις χωρὶς τῶν ἔργων
ἀργή ἐστιν; Ἀβραὰμ ὁ πατὴρ ἡμῶν οὐκ ἐξ ἔργων ἐδικαιώθη, 21
ἀνενέγκας Ἰςαὰκ τὸν γίον αγτογ ἐπὶ τὸ θγςιαςτήριον; βλέπεις ὅτι 22
ἡ πίστις συνήργει τοῖς ἔργοις αὐτοῦ καὶ ἐκ τῶν ἔργων ἡ πίστις
ἐτελειώθη, καὶ ἐπληρώθη ἡ γραφὴ ἡ λέγουσα Ἐπίςτεγςεν 23
δὲ Ἀβραὰμ τῷ θεῷ, καὶ ἐλογίςθη αγτῷ εἰς δικαιοσγνην, καὶ φίλος
θεογ ἐκλήθη. ὁρᾶτε ὅτι ἐξ ἔργων δικαιοῦται ἄνθρωπος καὶ 24
οὐκ ἐκ πίστεως μόνον. ὁμοίως δὲ καὶ Ῥαὰβ ἡ πόρνη οὐκ ἐξ 25
ἔργων ἐδικαιώθη, ὑποδεξαμένη τοὺς ἀγγέλους καὶ ἑτέρᾳ ὁδῷ
ἐκβαλοῦσα; ὥσπερ τὸ σῶμα χωρὶς πνεύματος νεκρόν ἐστιν, 26
οὕτως καὶ ἡ πίστις χωρὶς ἔργων νεκρά ἐστιν.

Μὴ πολλοὶ διδάσκαλοι γίνεσθε, ἀδελφοί μου, εἰδότες ὅτι ΙΙΙ
μεῖζον κρίμα λημψόμεθα· πολλὰ γὰρ πταίομεν ἅπαντες. εἴ 2
τις ἐν λόγῳ οὐ πταίει, οὗτος τέλειος ἀνήρ, δυνατὸς χαλινα-
γωγῆσαι καὶ ὅλον τὸ σῶμα. εἰ δὲ τῶν ἵππων τοὺς χαλινοὺς 3
εἰς τὰ στόματα βάλλομεν εἰς τὸ πείθεσθαι αὐτοὺς ἡμῖν,
καὶ ὅλον τὸ σῶμα αὐτῶν μετάγομεν. ἰδοὺ καὶ τὰ πλοῖα, 4
τηλικαῦτα ὄντα καὶ ὑπὸ ἀνέμων σκληρῶν ἐλαυνόμενα, μετά-
γεται ὑπὸ ἐλαχίστου πηδαλίου ὅπου ἡ ὁρμὴ τοῦ εὐθύνοντος

8   ΙΑΚΩΒΟΥ ΕΠΙΣΤΟΛΗ

5 βούλεται· οὕτως καὶ ἡ γλῶσσα μικρὸν μέλος ἐστὶν καὶ
6 μεγάλα αὐχεῖ. ἰδοὺ ἡλίκον πῦρ ἡλίκην ὕλην ἀνάπτει· καὶ ἡ
γλῶσσα πῦρ, ὁ κόσμος τῆς ἀδικίας ἡ γλῶσσα καθίσταται ἐν
τοῖς μέλεσιν ἡμῶν, ἡ σπιλοῦσα ὅλον τὸ σῶμα καὶ φλογίζουσα
τὸν τροχὸν τῆς γενέσεως καὶ φλογιζομένη ὑπὸ τῆς γεέννης.
7 πᾶσα γὰρ φύσις θηρίων τε καὶ πετεινῶν ἑρπετῶν τε καὶ
ἐναλίων δαμάζεται καὶ δεδάμασται τῇ φύσει τῇ ἀνθρωπίνῃ·
8 τὴν δὲ γλῶσσαν οὐδεὶς δαμάσαι δύναται ἀνθρώπων· ἀκατά-
9 στατον κακόν, μεστὴ ἰοῦ θανατηφόρου. ἐν αὐτῇ εὐλογοῦμεν
τὸν κύριον καὶ πατέρα, καὶ ἐν αὐτῇ καταρώμεθα τοὺς ἀνθρώ-
10 πους τοὺς καθ᾽ ὁμοίωσιν θεοῦ γεγονότας· ἐκ τοῦ αὐτοῦ στόματος
ἐξέρχεται εὐλογία καὶ κατάρα. οὐ χρή, ἀδελφοί μου, ταῦτα
11 οὕτως γίνεσθαι. μήτι ἡ πηγὴ ἐκ τῆς αὐτῆς ὀπῆς βρύει τὸ
12 γλυκὺ καὶ τὸ πικρόν; μὴ δύναται, ἀδελφοί μου, συκῆ ἐλαίας
ποιῆσαι ἢ ἄμπελος σῦκα; οὔτε ἁλυκὸν γλυκὺ ποιῆσαι ὕδωρ.
13 Τίς σοφὸς καὶ ἐπιστήμων ἐν ὑμῖν; δειξάτω ἐκ τῆς καλῆς
14 ἀναστροφῆς τὰ ἔργα αὐτοῦ ἐν πραΰτητι σοφίας. εἰ δὲ ζῆλον
πικρὸν ἔχετε καὶ ἐριθίαν ἐν τῇ καρδίᾳ ὑμῶν, μὴ κατακαυ-
15 χᾶσθε καὶ ψεύδεσθε κατὰ τῆς ἀληθείας. οὐκ ἔστιν αὕτη ἡ
σοφία ἄνωθεν κατερχομένη, ἀλλὰ ἐπίγειος, ψυχική, δαι-
16 μονιώδης· ὅπου γὰρ ζῆλος καὶ ἐριθία, ἐκεῖ ἀκαταστασία καὶ
17 πᾶν φαῦλον πρᾶγμα. ἡ δὲ ἄνωθεν σοφία πρῶτον μὲν ἁγνή
ἐστιν, ἔπειτα εἰρηνική, ἐπιεικής, εὐπειθής, μεστὴ ἐλέους
18 καὶ καρπῶν ἀγαθῶν, ἀδιάκριτος, ἀνυπόκριτος· καρπὸς δὲ
δικαιοσύνης ἐν εἰρήνῃ σπείρεται τοῖς ποιοῦσιν εἰρήνην.

IV   Πόθεν πόλεμοι καὶ πόθεν μάχαι ἐν ὑμῖν; οὐκ ἐντεῦθεν, ἐκ
τῶν ἡδονῶν ὑμῶν τῶν στρατευομένων ἐν τοῖς μέλεσιν ὑμῶν;
2 ἐπιθυμεῖτε, καὶ οὐκ ἔχετε· φονεύετε καὶ ζηλοῦτε, καὶ οὐ
δύνασθε ἐπιτυχεῖν· μάχεσθε καὶ πολεμεῖτε. οὐκ ἔχετε διὰ
3 τὸ μὴ αἰτεῖσθαι ὑμᾶς· αἰτεῖτε καὶ οὐ λαμβάνετε, διότι κακῶς
4 αἰτεῖσθε, ἵνα ἐν ταῖς ἡδοναῖς ὑμῶν δαπανήσητε. μοιχαλίδες,
οὐκ οἴδατε ὅτι ἡ φιλία τοῦ κόσμου ἔχθρα τοῦ θεοῦ ἐστίν; ὃς
ἐὰν οὖν βουληθῇ φίλος εἶναι τοῦ κόσμου, ἐχθρὸς τοῦ θεοῦ
5 καθίσταται. ἢ δοκεῖτε ὅτι κενῶς ἡ γραφὴ λέγει Πρὸς φθόνον
6 ἐπιποθεῖ τὸ πνεῦμα ὃ κατῴκισεν ἐν ἡμῖν; μείζονα δὲ δίδωσιν

χάριν· διὸ λέγει ΄Ο θεὸς ὑπερηφάνοις ἀντιτάσσεται ταπεινοῖς δὲ δίδωσιν χάριν. ᾿Υποτάγητε οὖν τῷ θεῷ· ἀντίστητε δὲ τῷ 7 διαβόλῳ, καὶ φεύξεται ἀφ᾿ ὑμῶν· ἐγγίσατε τῷ θεῷ, καὶ 8 ἐγγίσει ὑμῖν. καθαρίσατε χεῖρας, ἀμαρτωλοί, καὶ ἁγνίσατε καρδίας, δίψυχοι. ταλαιπωρήσατε καὶ πενθήσατε καὶ κλαύ- 9 σατε· ὁ γέλως ὑμῶν εἰς πένθος μετατραπήτω καὶ ἡ χαρὰ εἰς κατήφειαν· ταπεινώθητε ἐνώπιον Κυρίου, καὶ ὑψώσει ὑμᾶς. 10 Μὴ καταλαλεῖτε ἀλλήλων, ἀδελφοί· ὁ καταλαλῶν ἀδελφοῦ 11 ἢ κρίνων τὸν ἀδελφὸν αὐτοῦ καταλαλεῖ νόμου καὶ κρίνει νόμον· εἰ δὲ νόμον κρίνεις, οὐκ εἶ ποιητὴς νόμου ἀλλὰ κριτής. εἷς ἔστιν νομοθέτης καὶ κριτής, ὁ δυνάμενος σῶσαι καὶ ἀπο- 12 λέσαι· σὺ δὲ τίς εἶ, ὁ κρίνων τὸν πλησίον;

῎Αγε νῦν οἱ λέγοντες Σήμερον ἢ αὔριον πορευσόμεθα εἰς 13 τήνδε τὴν πόλιν καὶ ποιήσομεν ἐκεῖ ἐνιαυτὸν καὶ ἐμπορευσό- μεθα καὶ κερδήσομεν· οἵτινες οὐκ ἐπίστασθε τῆς αὔριον ποία 14 ἡ ζωὴ ὑμῶν· ἀτμὶς γάρ ἐστε πρὸς ὀλίγον φαινομένη, ἔπειτα καὶ ἀφανιζομένη· ἀντὶ τοῦ λέγειν ὑμᾶς ᾿Εὰν ὁ κύριος θέλῃ, 15 καὶ ζήσομεν καὶ ποιήσομεν τοῦτο ἢ ἐκεῖνο. νῦν δὲ καυχᾶσθε 16 ἐν ταῖς ἀλαζονίαις ὑμῶν· πᾶσα καύχησις τοιαύτη πονηρά ἐστιν. εἰδότι οὖν καλὸν ποιεῖν καὶ μὴ ποιοῦντι, ἁμαρτία 17 αὐτῷ ἐστίν. ῎Αγε νῦν οἱ πλούσιοι, κλαύσατε ὀλολύζοντες V ἐπὶ ταῖς ταλαιπωρίαις ὑμῶν ταῖς ἐπερχομέναις. ὁ πλοῦτος 2 ὑμῶν σέσηπεν, καὶ τὰ ἱμάτια ὑμῶν σητόβρωτα γέγονεν, ὁ 3 χρυσὸς ὑμῶν καὶ ὁ ἄργυρος κατίωται, καὶ ὁ ἰὸς αὐτῶν εἰς μαρτύριον ὑμῖν ἔσται καὶ φάγεται τὰς σάρκας ὑμῶν· ὡς πῦρ ἐθησαυρίσατε ἐν ἐσχάταις ἡμέραις. ἰδοὺ ὁ μισθὸς τῶν 4 ἐργατῶν τῶν ἀμησάντων τὰς χώρας ὑμῶν ὁ ἀφυστερημένος ἀφ᾿ ἡμῶν κράζει, καὶ αἱ βοαὶ τῶν θερισάντων εἰς τὰ ὦτα Κυρίου Σαβαὼθ εἰσελήλυθαν· ἐτρυφήσατε ἐπὶ τῆς γῆς καὶ ἐσπατα- 5 λήσατε, ἐθρέψατε τὰς καρδίας ὑμῶν ἐν ἡμέρᾳ σφαγῆς. κατε- 6 δικάσατε, ἐφονεύσατε τὸν δίκαιον. οὐκ ἀντιτάσσεται ὑμῖν;

Μακροθυμήσατε οὖν, ἀδελφοί, ἕως τῆς παρουσίας τοῦ 7 κυρίου. ἰδοὺ ὁ γεωργὸς ἐκδέχεται τὸν τίμιον καρπὸν τῆς

γῆς, μακροθυμῶν ἐπ᾽ αὐτῷ ἕως λάβῃ πρόϊμον καὶ ὄψιμον.
8 μακροθυμήσατε καὶ ὑμεῖς, στηρίξατε τὰς καρδίας ὑμῶν, ὅτι
9 ἡ παρουσία τοῦ κυρίου ἤγγικεν. μὴ στενάζετε, ἀδελφοί, κατ᾽
ἀλλήλων, ἵνα μὴ κριθῆτε· ἰδοὺ ὁ κριτὴς πρὸ τῶν θυρῶν
10 ἕστηκεν. ὑπόδειγμα λάβετε, ἀδελφοί, τῆς κακοπαθίας καὶ
τῆς μακροθυμίας τοὺς προφήτας, οἳ ἐλάλησαν ἐν τῷ ὀνόματι
11 Κυρίου. ἰδοὺ μακαρίζομεν τοὺϲ ὑπομείνανταϲ· τὴν ὑπομονὴν
Ἰὼβ ἠκούσατε, καὶ τὸ τέλος Κυρίου εἴδετε, ὅτι πολυ-
12 ϲπλαγχνόϲ ἐϲτιν ὁ κύριοϲ καὶ οἰκτίρμων.   Πρὸ πάντων
δέ, ἀδελφοί μου, μὴ ὀμνύετε, μήτε τὸν οὐρανὸν μήτε τὴν γῆν
μήτε ἄλλον τινὰ ὅρκον· ἤτω δὲ ὑμῶν τὸ Ναὶ ναὶ καὶ τὸ Οὔ
13 οὔ, ἵνα μὴ ὑπὸ κρίσιν πέσητε.   Κακοπαθεῖ τις ἐν ὑμῖν;
14 προσευχέσθω· εὐθυμεῖ τις; ψαλλέτω. ἀσθενεῖ τις ἐν ὑμῖν;
προσκαλεσάσθω τοὺς πρεσβυτέρους τῆς ἐκκλησίας, καὶ
προσευξάσθωσαν ἐπ᾽ αὐτὸν ἀλείψαντες ἐλαίῳ ἐν τῷ ὀνόματι
15 [τοῦ κυρίου]· καὶ ἡ εὐχὴ τῆς πίστεως σώσει τὸν κάμνοντα,
καὶ ἐγερεῖ αὐτὸν ὁ κύριος· κἂν ἁμαρτίας ᾖ πεποιηκώς, ἀφε-
16 θήσεται αὐτῷ. ἐξομολογεῖσθε οὖν ἀλλήλοις τὰς ἁμαρτίας
καὶ προσεύχεσθε ὑπὲρ ἀλλήλων, ὅπως ἰαθῆτε. πολὺ ἰσχύει
17 δέησις δικαίου ἐνεργουμένη. Ἡλείας ἄνθρωπος ἦν ὁμοιοπαθὴς
ἡμῖν, καὶ προσευχῇ προσηύξατο τοῦ μὴ βρέξαι, καὶ οὐκ
18 ἔβρεξεν ἐπὶ τῆς γῆς ἐνιαυτοὺς τρεῖς καὶ μῆνας ἕξ· καὶ πάλιν
προσηύξατο, καὶ ὁ οὐρανὸς ὑετὸν ἔδωκεν καὶ ἡ γῆ ἐβλάστησεν
19 τὸν καρπὸν αὐτῆς. Ἀδελφοί μου, ἐάν τις ἐν ὑμῖν πλανηθῇ
20 ἀπὸ τῆς ἀληθείας καὶ ἐπιστρέψῃ τις αὐτόν, γινώσκετε ὅτι ὁ
ἐπιστρέψας ἁμαρτωλὸν ἐκ πλάνης ὁδοῦ αὐτοῦ σώσει ψυχὴν
αὐτοῦ ἐκ θανάτου καὶ καλύψει πλῆθος ἁμαρτιῶν.

CHAPTER I

THE SUPERSCRIPTION

i. 1 'James, Servant of God and the Lord Jesus Christ, to the
Twelve Tribes of the Dispersion, greeting.'

In the terms of address every word is of moment. From the
form of salutation one inference alone seems possible, that the
Epistle purports to be the work of James, brother of the Lord,
who after the withdrawal of Peter succeeded to the headship of
the Christian believers in Jerusalem: and further that it is addressed not to a local or particular community, but to the more
general body of Jewish Christians—or it may be Christian Jews—
with whom his words would command a hearing. None other
could be denoted by the simple and authoritative '*James.*' Among
the original disciples, James son of Zebedee enjoyed a favoured
place, but his career was short-lived. 'In those days,' namely
while Barnabas and Saul were still engaged in building up the
Christian community at Antioch, in or about A.D. 44, 'Herod
the king stretched forth his hands against members of the Church
at Jerusalem, and made away with James the brother of John with
the sword' (A. xii. 1–2). He was first of the chosen Twelve
'to drink the cup,' and there is no evidence that he had attained
to any official position; except this brief chronicle of martyrdom,
there is no single reference to him in the Acts of the Apostles or
elsewhere, until he is laid hold of by the hagiologists; and except
for one or two unauthorised assumptions, no tradition associates
him with the Epistle.

Few names were commoner than James, i.e. Jacob; three
others occur in the Gospel narrative, James son of Alphæus,
one of the Twelve (Mk. iii. 18, Mt. x. 3, etc.), James the Little
(Mk. xv. 40, Mt. xxvii. 56), and James father of Judas—not
Iscariot—(L. vi. 16), but these are bare names, who left no
further trace in history or in tradition. Of James, 'brother of the
Lord,' the opposite is true. Apart from Paul and Peter, no figure

in the Church of the first days plays a more substantial part upon
the historic and the legendary stage than James, first 'Bishop'
of Jerusalem. That the Epistle *claims* to proceed from him seems
certain—and that claim won its way to gradual acceptance in
the West as well as in the East, and was probably a determining
factor in securing canonicity. The question for debate is whether
the ascription represents actual fact, or is the device of some later
Christian writer, who sheltered his modesty, or his ambitions,
under the ægis of an honoured name. In the absence of decisive
testimonia, the question can only be answered by internal evidences
of authenticity. The closest parallel is found in the salutation
'Judas, servant of Jesus Christ and brother of James,'[1] which
suggests that some such description as 'brother of the Lord' or
'brother of Jesus Christ' might have been adopted. In a later
writer, commending himself under an honoured name, that would
be natural, just as in 2 Peter we read 'Simon Peter, servant and
apostle of Jesus Christ'; but James would hardly have used it of
himself. His title to authority did not rest on bonds of con-
sanguinity, but on the suffrages of the community—Apostles,
presbyters and converts—to whom he owed his prerogative. No
official title is appended; so far as N.T. evidence is concerned,
there is no evidence that he was entitled either 'Bishop' or
'Apostle'; the terms so far as used of him were probably descriptive, and the latter would have been inappropriate to the resident
leader of the Church addressing those of the Dispersion; outside
the circle of the Twelve, 'Apostle' still carried much of its proper
sense as 'emissary.' The address seems only in keeping with one
whose name and person carried their own *imprimatur* to those
concerned. His claim to hearing rests not on official status, but
on divine commission similar to that conferred on the prophets
of old. Like Amos (iii. 7), like Zechariah (i. 6), he is numbered
among the '*servants of God.*' The term became a mandate of
trust, and it may be said of honour (as in Rev. x. 7), but in the
case of the writer it is delegated through '*the Lord Jesus Christ.*'

---

[1] Jude 1 Ἰούδας Ἰησοῦ Χριστοῦ δοῦλος ἀδελφὸς δὲ Ἰακώβου. It may
be observed that the terms Θεοῦ δοῦλος, Κύριος, and Χριστός were all of
Jewish origin, though early naturalised into the Christian vocabulary.

THE SUPERSCRIPTION 13

The designation Lord (*Kurios*) belongs to the vocabulary of the
Church of the first days in Jerusalem. In A. ii. 36 it is ascribed
to Peter even on the day of Pentecost: it is assumed in the earliest
Epistles of Paul[1]; and whatever subsequent extensions or ac-
cretions it may have gathered from Pagan cults or religions, it
owes its genesis to the Jewish Scriptures. Dogmatic values were
not as yet defined, but in the LXX *Kurios* was the accepted
equivalent for the Divine name, and the title of honour accorded
to moral authority derived from the Divine. The Lordship of
Jesus was the acknowledgment of his spiritual prerogative, even
as Christ was the recognition of his divine commission. There
could be no more succinct or pregnant description of James of
Jerusalem than '*servant of God, and of Lord—Jesus—the Christ.*'
On the exact implication and limits of the terms used regarding
Jesus Christ it will be better to defer discussion till we are prepared to deal with the Christology of the writer as a whole[2].
So far as his own title is concerned, the superscription stands
in a class by itself, not based on any local or institutional unity,
but on spiritual qualification of a specific kind. The appeal is to
'*the Twelve Tribes which are in the Dispersion.*' The twelve tribes
were no longer a political or ethnical unit; as such they had for
centuries ceased to exist, except for certain survival rights chiefly
connected with Judah, Benjamin and Levi. Their very names
and order are indeterminate; the twelve-tribe entity, the *dode-
caphylon* of A. xxvi. 7, had taken an established place in prophetic,
apocalyptic and symbolic phraseology, as denoting the commonwealth of Israel, that is the true spiritual Israel, in its completeness[3]. This was a recognised use which Paul could introduce with
propriety into his defence before Agrippa. Similarly in the Gospels
'the twelve tribes of Israel' are equivalent to 'the elect,'[4] the

[1] Gal. i. 3, vi. 14, 18, 1 Thes. i. 1, 3, 6, 8, and throughout the
Epistle.
[2] Chap. VIII. p. 88 f.
[3] Fully discussed by Zahn and Ropes *in loc.*
[4] Mt. xix. 28 ἐν τῇ παλινγενεσίᾳ ὅταν καθίσῃ ὁ υἱὸς τοῦ ἀνθρώπου ἐπὶ
θρόνου δόξης αὐτοῦ, καθήσεσθε καὶ ὑμεῖς ἐπὶ δώδεκα θρόνους κρίνοντες τὰς
δώδεκα φυλὰς τοῦ Ἰσραήλ—with which compare τοὺς ἐκλεκτούς Mk. xiii.
27 and Mt. xxiv. 31. The θρόνου δόξης illustrates foregoing.

whole body of the redeemed and spiritual Israel, who appear
as 'the twelve tribes of the sealed' in Apoc. vii. 4–8, as well as
in the twelve names inscribed upon the twelve gates of 'the holy
city descending out of heaven from God.'[1] The tradition is
carried on, and directly associated with the Messianic hope, in
apocalyptic writings such as the *Sibylline Oracles*[2], and the
Testaments of XII Patriarchs which have specially close affinities
with James. There can be no question that here it represents a
spiritual integer, and that the message is addressed to all faithful
Jews who are ready to accept the Messiahship, the teaching and
the service of Jesus as Lord. The effect of the word is simply
to contrast Jews of whatever locality—Jews as it were of the
dominions and colonies and possessions as compared with the
mother-country—with those who remained at the home-hearth,
the central seat of unity and the cradle of Christian Judaism. The
conception was at this era a familiar common-place, implicit in
Temple worship and the sacrificial system, in the Temple shekel,
and in the yearly festivals and pilgrimages—usages far more
realistic than Mecca can bring to bear upon the faith of Islam.

So understood, the superscription removes some difficulties
raised as to the precise character of the document, and the
absence of personal notes or greetings. It is not a letter sent to
correspondents and inviting answer; nor yet an occasional homily;
rather it is in the nature of a pastoral address or charge from one
in authority, conveying guidance, direction and encouragement to
the readers and setting forth the principles on which they rest;
it is the reduction to writing of conclusions, warnings and appeals,
which he strove constantly by precepts and example to drive
home. Difficulties about circulation at once disappear; means of
dissemination, formal or informal, were abundantly to hand; at
least as much so as for the circular mandate issued 'to the Gentile
brethren of Antioch and Syria and Cilicia' after the conference
at Jerusalem (A. xv. 23). And the term 'Dispersion' has its own

---

[1] Apoc. xxi. 12 ὀνόματα ἐπιγεγραμμένα ἅ ἐστι τῶν δώδεκα φυλῶν υἱῶν
Ἰσραήλ.
[2] *Sib. Oracl.* ii. 171 has ἡνίκα δωδεκάφυλος ἀπ' ἀντολίης λαὸς ἥξει
cf. iii. 249—but the epithet is no more than verbal illustration.

touch of pathos and appeal, as figuring the present condition and the beckoning hopes of those, who 'not having gotten the promises yet from afar off saw and greeted them' (Heb. xi. 13). Nor must it be forgotten that in relation to the church at Jerusalem the surrounding churches of Judæa, Samaria, Phœnicia, Damascus, Cyprus, Antioch and yet further afield, belonged in a specific sense to the Dispersion, which radiated from Jerusalem. Three times over the word is used of those who, in the persecution that followed the martyrdom of Stephen, had been 'dispersed' and driven into exile from the mother-church[1].

Thus the form of greeting fits perfectly the peculiar and indeed unique [2] position occupied by James, as head of the Christian body at Jerusalem, and defines with epigrammatic sureness the hearers, whom the words were intended to reach—not a particular or organised congregation, but the company of those who, repairing to the centre of the national faith, were prepared, whether from the Jewish or the Christian fold, to give ear to the message of Jesus, and through obedience to his teaching to qualify for the franchise of the spiritual Israel, and realise in him the fulfilment of the Messianic hope.

[1] A. viii. 1 πάντες δὲ διεσπάρησαν κατὰ τὰς χώρας τῆς Ἰουδαίας καὶ Σαμαρίας. viii. 4 οἱ μὲν οὖν διασπαρέντες διῆλθον. xi. 19 οἱ μὲν οὖν διασπαρέντες ἀπὸ τῆς θλίψεως τῆς γενομένης ἐπὶ Στεφάνῳ διῆλθον ἕως Φοινίκης καὶ Κύπρου καὶ Ἀντιοχείας.

[2] Well conceived and outlined, upon its merits, in Allen *Christian Institutions* p. 74.

CHAPTER II

PERSONALITY, CAREER AND SURROUNDINGS

Let us to begin with reconstitute the personality of James, so far
as data are available. Among the four brethren and two or more
sisters of the Lord, his name stands first, presumably as eldest.
As such he would enjoy the closest intimacy with Jesus during
the years of childhood and youth[1]. They were nurtured at one
mother's knee: learned from her lips no doubt that '*Blessed is the
man*,'[2] which became so dear a cadence to them both: shared
the disciplines of a devout God-fearing home, in which they were
brought up to strict observance of the Law, of Jewish rite and
rule, with that implicit and intimate reverence for the Scriptures,
which was the very atmosphere from which Jewish thought drew
breath. For thirty years and more they shared the village life
of Nazareth, and the favoured conditions which then prevailed
in Galilee[3]. Under the rule of Herod Antipas in Galilee and

[1] The implications of the Gospel narrative (Mt. i. 25, xiii. 54–6; L. ii. 7),
are decisive, and find something of corroboration in the tone and attitude
of the writer of the Epistle. In rejecting the Epiphanian hypothesis, of
children born to Joseph by an earlier marriage, there is no need to restate
the controversy. It is not vital to the main issues debated in this volume;
but it must sensibly affect the perspective of the reader, who desires to
realise the relations in which James stood to Jesus, to Peter, to Paul, and
to others of his contemporaries. The Epiphanian contention, in deference
to doctrinal and ascetic prepossessions, sets aside the literary evidence
and maintains the perpetual virginity of Mary. But it also introduces
chronological results, which have not as yet received the attention they
deserve. The year 8 or 7 B.C. is gaining general acceptance as the probable
date of the Nativity. Upon the Epiphanian showing, this would throw
back the birth of James (as eldest of six or more children of a previous
union) to 15 or 14 B.C. *at latest*. His martyrdom took place in A.D. 62,
so that we must picture him as nearing eighty, if not more, at the time
of his death. There is nothing in the records to suggest so advanced an
age; nor does it find support from the general impression conveyed by
the Book of Acts in describing his relations with Paul and others.

[2] i. 12, derived from Ps. i. 1, xxxiv. 8, xl. 5, etc., and recurrent in the
Beatitudes.

[3] For detailed evidences, compare Farrar *Early Days of Christianity*

Peræa (4 B.C.—A.D. 39), and still more of his brother Philip as tetrarch (4 B.C.—A.D. 34) of Trachonitis, Ituræa and the adjoining trans-Jordanic regions which included the cities of the Decapolis, all Northern Palestine enjoyed a golden age of prosperity and peace, virtually unbroken by casual seditions or external war. The rich tableland of Galilee, and not least the plain and lake-side of Gennesaret, were on the immemorial route by which the eastern convoys from the Euphrates and Damascus gained access to the Mediterranean ports of Tyre, Sidon or Joppa, and at the head of the Jordan valley held a place of vantage upon the great thoroughfare which connected Antioch and Syria in the North with Arabia and Egypt in the South. At the sources of the Jordan, on the southern foothills of Mt Hermon, Philip planted his new and splendid capital Cæsarea Philippi, and at its outgoings into the Lake of Galilee, transformed Bethsaida, 'the home of fishers,' into the populous city of Julias. Similarly, Herod rebuilt Sepphoris at the cross-roads a few miles north of Nazareth, and a little later created Tiberias on the west shore of the lake as his official metropolis, surrounding his palace there with places of worship, baths, mansions and colonnades on a scale of sumptuous magnificence. While flowing streams of commerce yielded a royal revenue, taxation was proportionately light, and the surpassing fertility of the soil in this 'garden of the earth,' the orchards of olive, fig and grape, the corn-lands, and the inexhaustible supply of fish, turned the whole lake-basin into a hive of prosperous industries; with not more than his usual extravagance in statistics, Josephus in less happy days computes the population of Galilee at 3,000,000, and credits it with numbers of cities and townships, the least of which contained upwards of 15,000 inhabitants[1]. Among these Nazareth would count for one

pp. 272, 285–7, G. A. Smith *Hist. Geog. of Holy Land* Chap. xx, Headlam *Life and Teaching of Jesus Christ* 55, 98 pp.

[1] In Jos. *Vita* § 45 the total of cities and townships (πόλεις καὶ κῶμαι) is set down at 204. On these figures, combined from Jos. *B.J.* II. x. 7–8, etc., III. iii and x, see Merrill *Galilee in the Time of Christ*, G. A. Smith *Hist. Geog.* p. 421, Headlam *Life and Teaching* pp. 99, 172 Klausner p. 261.

2

while at Taricheæ alone at the foot of the lake the able-bodied inhabitants exceeded 30,000. In miniature the 'multitudes' (e.g. Mk. iii. 7–9, Mt. viii. 1, xix. 2, etc.) who flocked to the teaching of Jesus confirm the picture, and such were the conditions that attended his ministry, and amid which James passed from youth to manhood.

The one incident in which James enters the Gospel narrative is in keeping with that which is to follow. Among the figures of the Apostolic age, James is the most tenaciously conservative: and when at the outset of his ministry Jesus broke with the orthodox tradition, challenged the authority of Rabbis, Scribes and Pharisees, presumed to question the enactments of the Law, consorted with publicans and sinners, declared the Son of Man lord also of the Sabbath, and proclaimed the coming of the Kingdom in terms of catastrophic change, James could put no other interpretation on his conduct than 'He is beside himself' (Mk. iii. 21). That one of their own household, a fellow-workman at the bench, should be 'the Christ' must have seemed a staggering impossibility, a claim not to be entertained, unscriptural and revolutionary. To the last 'his brethren believed not on him' (J. vii. 5), and sought only to save him from his own delusions (Mt. xii. 46, Mk. iii. 31, L. viii. 19, J. vii. 3–9).

There is no further note of contact, until in St Paul's brief recapitulation (1 Cor. xv. 7) we read, 'After that' (the appearance to the 500) 'he was seen of James.' Where Scripture does not furnish even a hint, conjecture is worse than useless. Is it not true to say that each recorded appearance is in the nature of a surprise? The *Gospel of the Hebrews*, seemingly among the most impressive of apocryphal compilations, does indeed introduce a scene and dialogue not ill-composed; but it is no more than a descant upon a Gospel text (Mk. xiv. 25). One thing alone seems sure, that the appearance was for James himself decisive. Forthwith, in company with the women from Galilee, Mary the mother and his brethren, he joined the inner circle of the disciples (A. i. 13–14), shared with them the days of prayerful expectation, the Pentecostal outpouring of the Spirit, and the years of infant development and growth. As yet leadership rested with Peter and John; but when three years after his conversion[1] Paul re-visited Jerusalem, Peter excepted, he conferred only 'with James the brother of the Lord' (Gal. i. 18–19). The years confirmed his spiritual title, and when A.D. 46 Paul went up with Barnabas from Antioch to receive their commission to the Gentiles (Gal. ii. 9), he actually gives first place among the three chief 'pillars' of the Church—James, Peter and John—to the name of James[2]. Be that as it may, when the execution of James the son of Zebedee and the imprisonment and withdrawal of Peter broke up and dispersed the Apostolic band, James as of natural right succeeded to the leadership, and there at the central shrine, the mother-city of the Church of Christ, continued stedfast in the faith, until he too in his turn, like Stephen and like James the son of Zebedee, became the victim of religious hate.

At this stage, the centre of action for the writer of the Acts shifts from Jerusalem to the missionary enterprises of Paul. But as the drama widens, and new scenes and issues complicate the plot, side-lights are flashed from time to time upon the attitude of James to Gentile and to Jewish Christianity. When first the evangelisation of the Gentile world was broached, James was foremost in holding out 'right hands of fellowship to Paul and Barnabas' (Gal. ii. 9). His own mission indeed was 'to the circumcision'; in personal practice he adhered to the prescriptive ceremonies and tabus, as well as to the ritual obligations, of Jewish law; 'certain which came from James' (Gal. ii. 12) represented him, perhaps not dishonestly, as opposed to any kind of relaxation. But when the issue was raised, and fresh from their missionary triumphs Paul and Barnabas submitted their appeal 'to the apostles and the elders' at Jerusalem (A.xv.2–4), James, seconding the appeal of Peter (A. xv. 13 ff.), threw the full weight of his

---

[1] The date of the Conversion is very disputable, i.e. from A.D. 33 to 36. Knox associates the execution of Stephen with the recall of Pilate to Rome in 35, and the temporary abeyance of procuratorship. This postpones the Conversion to A.D. 36, when Aretas was in occupation of Damascus.
[2] This may be due only to later events; or even to avoid confusion from a coupling of his name with John. Whether others of the Twelve were at Jerusalem the verse gives no indication.

influence upon the side of Gentile immunities from the yoke of Jewish rigorism, not excepting the rite of circumcision itself. As at their first start, 'remember the poor' (Gal. ii. 10) had been his parting benediction, so now to him the criterion of conduct[1], of spiritual fruits, of Christian behaviour and fellowship, were sufficient to weigh down the scale. Apart from moral determinants he was ready to accept such compromises, ceremonial, institutional or disciplinary, as served best to meet or relieve the situation. The resolutions, which he submitted to the conference, were of a makeshift kind, and neither their exact purport or range of application is clear. They are more concerned with conduct than with principle: but at the cost of a harmless concession, they saved the bond of Christian brotherhood and freedom.

The occasion of Paul's last visit to Jerusalem (A. xxi. 18 ff.), shows the same spirit working from the opposite direction. To conciliate and disabuse the zealots, James proposed that Paul should in the Temple publicly discharge the obligations of a ceremonial[2] vow, and should on behalf of four poor Christians take on himself the cost of the legal charges and ritual sacrifices which the performance of such vows entailed. The incidents, though disconnected, yield a consistent whole, and reveal a temper and personality with which the main tenor of the Epistle, alike in its utterances and its reticences, falls into natural accord. It has been impugned as religious opportunism. But the spirit of Christian tolerance, one may almost say of statesmanship, lies always open to that charge; and it was of the essence of Judaic Christianity.

The reform on which James pinned his hopes was ethical: he stands in the succession of the prophets—of Amos and Micah, of John the Baptist and Jesus—as a pleader for *righteousness*. Apart from ethical demands he sought no new departures in doctrine or in worship. He built upon the Hebrew Scriptures, adhered

---

[1] The case is at its strongest, if the Codex D omission of καὶ πνικτοῦ in A. xv. 20, 29 is accepted, and the prohibitions comprise only 'idolatry,' 'fornication' and 'blood-shedding.'

[2] The exact obligations of the vow at Cenchreæ (A. xviii. 18), or of the votive purifications at Jerusalem (A. xxi. 24–6) do not appear, but they involved public and ritual compliance with the hieratic regulations.

to the traditions of the fathers; worshipping in the Temple, keeping feast and fast, loyal to the constituted order, trusting by precept and example to win the twelve tribes of the reborn and spiritual Israel into a united Christian brotherhood[1]. In the Epistle it is often hard to say whether the writer is addressing himself to Christian or to Jew; the language and thought accommodate themselves to both, because to the author each God-fearing Jew was a potential or an actual Christian. In this natural blend of Jewish piety and Christian consecration lay the qualification for leadership, which enabled him for twenty years, A.D. 42–62, to preside over the Church at Jerusalem, and to command the reverence of all Jewish Christians or Christian Jews, who flocked thither in attendance on the annual festivals, or on pilgrimage to the sacred city of the Lord. His ascendancy was that of personal holiness: that is the consentient testimony of the whole body of posthumous literature which canonised his memory—the solid background on which all the embroideries of legend were wrought. When we read[2] that he was a Nazirite from his mother's womb, that wine and strong drink never passed his lips, that (like the Ebionites) he abstained from all flesh food, that by special privilege he had access to the holy place, the colouring is obviously that of partisan and interested sects; even in statements that he was surnamed 'the Righteous,' 'James the Just,' that his garb was scanty and austere, that with incessant prayer his knees grew gnarled like a camel's, that he received from the hand of Jesus the sacramental bread of brotherhood[3], the treatment may be impressionist rather than photographic; but all alike concur in centring the emphasis on personal sanctity as the indelible impression bequeathed to his successors by the

[1] ἀδελφοί is the reiterated term of address, occurring sixteen times in the Epistle, see p. 34 n.
[2] Mainly from Hegesippus as quoted in Eusebius *H.E.* ii. 23. Burkitt *Christian Beginnings* p. 57 ff., and still more unreservedly Klausner *Jesus of Nazareth* p. 41–2, is disposed to accept these traits as authentic, describing James as 'one of the most ardent advocates of the Jewish written and oral Law.' But this is not borne out by N.T., or Josephus, or by our Epistle, in which Klausner builds on ii. 10: and, in the particulars adduced, later Ebionite (or similar) colouring seems unmistakeable.
[3] *Gospel of the Hebrews* as cited by Jerome *De Vir. Illustr.* 2.

personality of James. So with the story of his death; details may disagree or be confused—the pinnacle, the Temple steps, the braining with the fuller's club[1]—but the charge alleged is one with that levelled against Jesus himself, and the words of dying forgiveness are an echo from the Cross. Even among the ecclesiastical ramifications of the later Clementine romances, the old note of personal sanctity remains dominant. He is of the type familiar to the East, the Holy Man—*fakir* or *sadhu*—whose authority rested upon devout asceticism and uncompromising holiness of personal life. But in ascetic consecration he did not hold aloof from social contacts. He lived always at the centre, bearing witness by example more than precept, never dissociated from Jerusalem, the metropolis and the great pilgrim magnet of the Jewish faith. There amid kaleidoscopic changes and the whirl of conflicting currents, in a society torn with intrigue, faction and dispute, and disintegrated by religious feuds, he stood for righteousness, refraining to the utmost from controversy, and labouring for goodwill and peace.

His own affinities by training and by instinct were with the Pharisees; in the computation of Josephus he would have been included among the 6000 whom he assigns to that persuasion. But the term Pharisee denotes no strict or homogeneous unity, of creed or practice: it comprehends all those who in observance and belief clung to the authority of the Law as the divine and binding pledge of national unity and survival, as the badge and privilege of the covenanted people. But within the fold, the sacred hedge of the Law, there was room for wide divergence of opinion. Over the whole field the rival schools of Hillel and of Shammai kept up their running conflict: among the Pharisees were legalists, apocalyptists, Messianists, Scribes and Rabbis, priests and politicians, simple pietists and fierce rigorists, moralists and hypocrites. Schools of thought, parties, shades of opinion were as wide apart as in the Church of England, or the yet wider complex known as Unitarian. Nicodemus repairing to Jesus by night, Joseph of Arimathæa providing burial for him whom colleagues of his own had crucified, Gamaliel the Master pleading

[1] Clem. Alex. *ap*. Euseb. *H.E.* ii. 1.

PERSONALITY, CAREER AND SURROUNDINGS 23

for non-intervention (A. v. 35–9), Saul the disciple yet breathing
out threatenings and slaughters (A. ix. 1), all furnish typical
contrasts. The Pharisees were scrupulous observants of the
ceremonial system; but the direction and ritual of the Temple
were in the hands of their opponents. Hardly an attribute or
belief can be predicated of Pharisees which does not admit of
reasoned contradiction. Their own effective organ of propaganda
was the synagogue. They held of course no monopoly: but they
were constant in attendance, occupied chief seats[1], and largely
controlled the conduct of worship, as masters of ceremonies,
upholders of disciplines, leaders of devotions, and contributors
to debate. Naturally, it is the one organisation recognised by
James (ii. 2), just as Paul found in it the primary instrument for
his missionary propaganda. And the constitution of the synagogue, in its origins Palestinian, was congregational, Hebraic,
Hellenic, Alexandrine as the case might be[2], and common to the
whole range of the Dispersion.

To realise that James was a Pharisee is important and instructive, though always subject to the proviso that this yields no
precise definition of doctrine or of ecclesiastical policy. Pharisaism
found expression in sharply contrasted phases and sections; nowhere more so than in the Galilæan surroundings in which James
was brought up. Among the Pharisean zealots devotion to Torah
demanded irreconcileable recalcitrance; armed revolt was a sacred
duty to those who were called 'to seize by force the Kingdom of
God,'[3] and by thousands and tens of thousands they threw down
their desperate challenge to the unbeliever. To the Quietist
groups on the other hand the same devotion imposed abstinence
from political and secular attempts[4]. They were 'the meek of
the earth,' passivists whose ideal lay in submission, and waiting
upon God, whose Messianic hope was bound up with belief in
a future life. It was to this wing that Jesus and his family belonged—a carpenter, 'the son of a carpenter'—and in loyalty

[1] The Scribes of Mk. ii. 16 were 'Scribes of the Pharisees.'
[2] See further, p. 26.
[3] Klausner *Jesus of Nazareth* pp. 202–6, following Chwolson.
[4] Klausner pp. 121–3, 171–3.

to this tradition James remained a resolute and conscientious pacifist to the end[1].

This variety of phase in Pharisaism has left its mark upon the pages of the Synoptic Gospels. In Mark their representatives, described as 'the Scribes of the Pharisees, appear in the synagogue as the official custodians of the national faith, the experts whose duty it was to question the credentials and on occasion to take exception to the declarations of Jesus; but beyond this, neither recriminations nor persecution are alleged in the Galilæan ministry. There is nothing to correspond with the collective denunciations, still less with the Philippic of indictment, which Matthew embodies in the Seven Woes uttered at Jerusalem (Mt. xxiii). These take their colour in part from the final breach with Rabbinism, that is to say with the militant extremists of the Shammai school, who captured and voiced the Pharisaic platform at Jerusalem at the period to which the Gospel belongs. Even throughout the final scenes of the betrayal, the trial and the crucifixion, Mark refrains from any collective indictment, and throughout introduces the Pharisees under the term 'the elders,' implicating only their official representatives in the Sanhedrin. The line taken by James is closely parallel with that adopted in St Mark. It was his fate to be done to death[2] by national extremists, who resented his protests against violence; but to the Pharisees and friends of moderation he owed honourable burial on the site of his martyrdom, and their protests addressed to King Agrippa and the Roman Procurator (Albinus) procured the summary deposition of the Sadducean High Priest.

[1] Lechler i. 65–6.
[2] See pp. 116–117.

CHAPTER III

JAMES AND HIS READERS

The surroundings in which James and his fellow-Christians moved differed widely from those of the Hellenic churches, founded and portrayed by St Paul. Alike on the lineal and on the environmental side, reactions to Judaism, not to Paganism, determined their development. And except in incidents connected with Paul—the stoning of Stephen and the Conversion—the author of the Acts shows little of the selective clarity and grasp exhibited in his account of the missionary journeys. But at least the general features of the situation are made clear. The first believers were not conscious of any open or deliberate breach with Judaism; they disclaimed none of the requirements of the Mosaic Law or of established custom (A. x. 14); the Law, the Prophets, and the Messianic hope were part of their spiritual birthright; adhering to the example set by Jesus himself, their attendance at the Temple, their observance of feast and sacrifice was exemplary (A. ii. 46, iii. 1. 11, v. 12. 42, xxi. 20, xxii. 17); they questioned none of the prerogatives of the ruling hierarchy. The record is explicit—'Having favour with all the people' (ὅλον τὸν λαόν A. ii. 47) '....the number of disciples multiplied exceedingly, and *a great mass* (ὄχλος) *of the priests* gave ear to the faith' (vi. 7)[1]. They did not even profess or preach a 'pure and reformed' Judaism; they were but one additional 'persuasion' or 'following,'[2] who were content simply to add to the fundamental beliefs and observances of Judaism the conviction that the expected Messiah had appeared in the person of Jesus, coupled with a pledge of abiding allegiance to his person and his teaching. The conception and the attributes of the Messiah remained hardly less fluid than before.

---

[1] Lechler i. 70 goes too far in claiming 'high favour with the whole population of Jerusalem'; it is a question of tolerance and sympathy on the part of the ruling sects.

[2] αἵρεσις (A. xxiv. 5, 14) and ὁδός (A. ix. 2) are terms used in Acts.

Neither were they Separatists. The constitution of the synagogue allowed almost unlimited latitude in matters of religious opinion. The conduct of worship[1] was not regulated by a central or even an organised ministry, but by the chief or 'ruler of the synagogue' (Mk. v. 22, 35–8, L. viii. 41, 49, A. xviii. 8, 17, etc.), who at his discretion committed the reading of the books, or the leading in prayer, to whom he willed. Visitors could be invited to officiate, as in the case of Jesus and of Paul, and strangers were admitted as well as proselytes[2]. The picture of Jas. ii. 2—' *If there come into your synagogue* (gathering, rather than building) *a man with a gold ring, in gay apparel*'—is true to the current usage; it is not aimed at a particular congregation, but was an incident, used for illustration, that might happen any day in Jerusalem itself or throughout the Dispersion[3]. And there was hardly any limit to the number of synagogues: ten was laid down as the lower limit to form a 'gathering,' and there was even the smaller and more informal unit of the 'Prayer' ($\pi\rho o\sigma\epsilon\upsilon\chi\acute{\eta}$) or prayer-meeting, of which we read at Philippi and elsewhere (A. xvi. 13, 16); thus synagogues abounded in Rome, in the time of Augustus[4], and at Jerusalem (which was exceptional) we read of as many as 300 or 400, prior to the final siege. Each little group formed a 'gathering' of its own, so that there were synagogues (A. vi. 9) of Alexandrians, Cyrenians, Cilicians, of the Libertines, and others, drawn together by natural affinities. A separate synagogue of Christian believers, if formed, would not lie under any stigma of schism or non-conformity. Their one special rite, 'the breaking of bread,' was associated with domestic gatherings and the common meal, not with synagogue worship. They had inevitably to endure the sneers and the reproaches, the social slights and disabilities, to which obscure eccentrics are exposed in any prejudiced

[1] For a careful study of Synagogue procedure, see Abrahams *Studies in Pharisaism* I. pp. 1–15. For various uses of the word applied to Christian or Judæo-Christian congregations see Zahn i. 94–5.

[2] Cf. 1 Cor. xiv.

[3] Nowhere in N.T. is $\sigma\upsilon\nu\alpha\gamma\omega\gamma\acute{\eta}$ used of the specifically Christian gathering. Later, especially in Judæan churches, the term was occasionally admitted. The closest N.T. parallel is the descriptive $\dot{\epsilon}\pi\iota\sigma\upsilon\nu\alpha\gamma\omega\gamma\acute{\eta}$ of Heb. x. 25.

[4] Philo *Leg. ad Gaium* § 23.

society, but beyond these—though the eye of the Rulers, the Elders, the Scribes and the Priests was upon them (A. iv. 5–6, 23, v. 17)—they did not incur overt or official persecution, until they came into conflict with the pretensions and the policy of the ruling caste: upon the ethical side, from the first, they found active sympathisers among the priests (A. vi. 7), and supporters such as Gamaliel (A. v. 34), even among the leading and official Pharisees. Distrust was chiefly directed against the Hellenist section, who claimed rights of self-determination, which threatened disruption of the nationalist polity. At the trial of Stephen, it was not so much his criticism of the Law or even his forecast of the ruin of the Temple that roused the ire of the Sanhedrin, as his denunciation of the narrowness and bigotry of the nationalist leaders (A. vii. 51). His stoning was an act of religious lynching by the 'patriot' party of violence, who seized upon his protests as a handle for open and wholesale terrorism, and for extinction of those claims to independence, religious as well as administrative, which he had championed[1] (A. vi. 1). On the death of Stephen large numbers, in fear for their person or their property, fled for refuge to Samaria (A. viii. 5, 25) or Galilee, to Philistia and the desert country of the South (A. viii. 26), or yet further afield, to Antioch or to Damascus, though the Apostles themselves, it would seem (A. viii. 14, ix. 27, xi. 1) still clung to Jerusalem and there pursued their Christian propaganda: but the rapid growth of converts, emphasised no doubt by reports from Antioch and elsewhere, was enough to kindle the jealous alarm of their opponents, who finally induced Herod to initiate a policy of open violence, to put James brother of John to the sword, and cast Peter the leader into prison. The imprisonment was the natural sequel to his new departure in admitting Cornelius to Christian communion, without enforcing the requirements of the Jewish

[1] Orthodox dislike of the Hellenists may be illustrated from the scornful sarcasm of J. vii. 35—'Whither will this man go that we shall not find him? Will he go unto the Dispersion of the Greeks, and teach the Greeks?' The blight of racial prejudice, the canker of central Judaism, was a leading factor in the final rejection of Christ, and determined the destinies of Christianity as a Gentile faith. The Dispersion received the Christ, whom the seed of Abraham rejected.

Law. This made his position at Jerusalem no longer tenable; to
Jewish rigorists he had become not merely suspect, but an open
traitor to the cause. A few months later, after the death of Herod,
he does indeed appear at Jerusalem, pleading with whatever
reservations the claims of Gentile immunities, but already occu-
pying a secondary place, and henceforward whether at Antioch,
in Asia, or elsewhere, his Apostleship is associated with churches
of Gentile as well as Jewish composition[1]. At Jerusalem—with
the express approval, if Clement of Alexandria is to be trusted,
of Peter and of John—the leadership was vested in James the
brother of the Lord.

Alike on the personal and the official side his position was
exceptional. His unshorn locks, his sparse attire, his unremitting
disciplines of public prayer, made him a notable and picturesque
figure at the central shrine: none could question his consistency
of life, his devoutness in observance, his fidelity to the traditions
of Israel, his passionate desire for religious unity and peace; and
his rigorous asceticism exempted him from some of the contentions [2]—respecting meats, drinks and sacrifice—which gave
rise to bitter disputes between rival Jewish sects, as well as
between Jew and Gentile.

More than this: in the heart of every Jew Jerusalem held its
place not as a military stronghold or as an emporium of commerce,
but as the divinely appointed capital and centre of the chosen
people's destinies. And to the 'twice-born' Israel it was hallowed
with a yet higher consecration, as the cradle of the Christian faith,
the scene of the Crucifixion, the Resurrection and the Ascension,
and thereafter the focus of the Apostolic activities, and the central
hearth from which the Christian communities, not only of Galilee,
Syria and the East, but also all Western Christendom, derived
the sacred fire. As mother-church of all the churches [3], Jerusalem
enjoyed a primacy, with which none other could compare; and

[1] 'It is one of the mistakes of the Tübingen school that it did not
recognise that Peter, not only in the Acts but also in the Pauline Epistles,
is on the Hellenistic not the Hebrew side,' Foakes Jackson and Lake
Beginnings of Christianity i. 312.
[2] Burkitt *Christian Beginnings* 57 ff.
[3] Gal. iv. 26, 'Jerusalem which is from above..., the mother of us all.'

this primacy was reflected in James, as its revered official head. Up to the time of his death, the church at Jerusalem remained central, the fountain-head of Christendom[1]. It was no question of ecclesiastical status: terms like Diocesan or Metropolitan Bishop are importations from the third century (or later) from which the Clementine romances date. In the preliminary letters (later in date) to the Clementine Homilies, James is saluted by Peter as 'Lord and Bishop of the Holy Church,' is styled 'Bishop of Bishops' in rivalry with Rome; or as in *Clem. Recog.* I. 68–73, is denoted as 'Arch-priest' or 'Archbishop,' a title nowhere else current before the fourth century. But as writer of the Epistle, '*James*' claims no titular or territorial jurisdiction. His commission as '*servant of God and the Lord Jesus Christ*' was a sphere of influence co-extensive with those who looked to Jerusalem as the fountain-head and centre of the faith. Their number is wholly indeterminate: we read of 3000 baptised at the first Pentecost (A. ii. 41); a little later of 5000 added to the Church (A. iv. 4); and subsequently of disciples, crowds and churches 'multiplied exceedingly' in Jerusalem (A. vi. 7), described in A. xxi. 20 as 'tens of thousands, all zealous for the law.' But these round figures[2] and general terms do not represent an organised unit; nor do they include the outlying churches (A. viii. 1, ix. 31) or the mixed multitudes who, at the yearly feasts, resorted to Jerusalem, and who without committing themselves to ties of formal

[1] It is now generally admitted that it was in the churches of Palestine and Syria that the term 'Bishop' first passed from a descriptive to a titular designation, marking a differentiation between him and the general body of presbyters. And this was partly due to the transitional and unique position, occupied by James as leader and head of the Christian body at Jerusalem. Cf. Headlam *Church and Reunion* p. 73, where the terms 'Christian high priest' and 'Sanhedrin' do not seem happy, and Scott *First Age of Christianity* p. 161.

[2] The round figures of Josephus are a warning in numerical statistics: 3,000,000 in Jerusalem for the last Passover, over 20,000 killed in one hour at Cæsarea, more than 100,000 in his own Galilæan army, 8500 dead bodies in the Court of the Temple, followed by the execution of 12,000 of the better sort, as the result of the Idumæan raid into Jerusalem, are among his fancy totals (Knox *St Paul and Church of Jerusalem* p. 15, n. 21). So again 'Among the numerous villages or townships of Galilee, the very least contains over 15,000 inhabitants.' See p. 17 note.

membership came under the influence of Christian teaching, and who, impressed by the arresting personality of James, by his kinship with Jesus and by his accepted leadership, leaned on his utterances for directive guidance and inspiration. For all these composite elements there could be no better description than '*the twelve tribes in the dispersion*' of the spiritual Israel, to whom his message was addressed.

If such be the true setting of the Epistle, it is only natural that there should be no appeal to Christian baptism, nor to specific forms of worship—whether Jewish sacrifice on the one hand, or the Eucharistic 'breaking of bread' on the other. Any such reference to institutional or ceremonial practices is precluded by the same conditions as hold good of the doctrinal teaching: the attitude is broadly comprehensive, designed to win disciples to Jesus as the Christ.

This is the sufficient answer to those who regard the Epistle as addressed to a particular church or congregation. The passages on which they rely convict them of a strange lack of literary perception, and all make for a contrary conclusion. In his protest against unchristian '*respect of persons*' (ii. 2) James introduces his lively illustration '*If there come into your gathering* (συναγωγήν) *a man with a gold ring, in gay apparel*' (ii. 2). The picture is a true and telling type, such as might occur in a 'Character' of Theophrastus or of Hall, and has plentiful parallels in the pages of the O.T. prophets and moralists. To suppose that James is here pillorying the directors of a particular congregation, or some well-to-do frequenter of their little gathering, verges on the ridiculous. Again, the vehement outburst of iv. 1—'*Whence wars, and whence battles among you?*' is adduced. The words used (πόλεμοι καὶ μάχαι) are not applicable to the disagreements and quarrels of a congregation: they refer to the fierce and murderous affrays, the 'wars and battles'[1] of rival religious factions with

---

[1] The literal sense is riveted on them by φονεύετε..., μάχεσθε καὶ πολεμεῖτε of the following verse; and gives the clue to the right interpretation of ἐθρέψατε τὰς καρδίας ὑμῶν ἐν ἡμέρᾳ σφαγῆς, which does not mean 'gorging your appetite,' but 'nursing your souls' (v. 5), that is, taking delight in and gloating over sanguinary reprisals. See further, pp. 85 and 113.

which the *Antiquities*[1] and *Jewish War* of Josephus are filled. A third passage cited is that in which once again the writer takes up his parable against the extortions and extravagances of mis-used wealth—'*The hire of the labourers who mow your lands, which is of you kept back by fraud, crieth; and the outcries of them that reap have entered into the ears of the Lord of Sabaoth*' (v. 4). This is no personal attack on wealthy individuals of a congregation, but the exposure of a rampant social evil. By reason of the vehemence of the attack, the terms and the illustration are highly generalised: the passage may be almost described as a *cento* of phrases and excerpts from the prophets. The excesses of the plutocrats and profiteers of Jerusalem are in the forefront of the writer's mind, and the heat of indignation recalls the cleansing of the Temple, but he prefers to illustrate from the sufferings of the rural population, who were among the victims and indeed formed the main bulk of his readers[1].

Thus the illustrations employed combine to show the breadth and realism of his appeal. The first, in consonance with the actual state of things, treats 'the synagogue'—the gathering that is of early believers—as the sphere in which the law of love ought to prevail. The second calls in evidence the social and political discords against which it has to make good. The third pleads the cause of the peasant, poor and downtrodden, against the greed and the exactions of the usurer. By tradition and antecedents the Palestinian Jews were a nation of agriculturists. The one great town, Jerusalem, was sustained as the centre of worship and of pilgrimage, by the contributions of the peasantry. The golden age of Maccabæan independence is described in these terms—'They tilled their land in peace, and the land gave her increase, and the trees of the plains their fruits.... They sat each man under his vine and his fig-tree, and there was none to make them afraid.'[2] The grinding burdens of taxation, imperial and local, which

---

[1] For the particular period, see Jos. *Ant.* xx. v–vi. In *B.J.* II. xiii. 2 Josephus writes of Eleazar the arch-robber who had ravaged the country for twenty years, and under date A.D. 52, 'So the robbers returned to their strongholds, and thenceforward all Judæa was infested with brigandage.' *Ant.* xx. vi. 1.

[2] 1 Macc. xiv. 8, 12.

resulted from the Syrian and later from Roman domination fell
with crushing weight upon the peasantry and drove them into
the activities of expatriated traders and small vendors. Im-
poverishment and chronic insecurity dispossessed the small-
holders of their freeholds, which fell into the hands of a small
knot of moneyed owners and rack-renters, who rallied round the
Sadducean aristocracy. These are the real objects of the writer's
denunciation; and as a mark of time it should be noted that these
economic conditions, the day of large land-holders preying upon
a burdened peasantry, came to an end with the Jewish War, and
point decisively to an earlier date.

Another expostulation (iv. 13–14) turns the searchlight upon
the traders and commercial middlemen—so characteristic an
element among the itinerating Jews—who in their restless pursuit
of gain keep no thought of God before their eyes. Thus passage
after passage answers to the known features and conditions of
contemporary Jewish life, though it is inept to regard the poor and
the purse-proud, the peasant and the land-holder, the voluptuary
and the skin-flint, the capitalist and the bagman, as associated
in a single group or congregation. The second-person form of
address, the reiterated ' *You* ' varies with the class addressed, just
as it does in the First Epistle General of Peter, which in this (as
in other) respects furnishes the nearest parallel. It is the only
form suitable to the prophet-preacher. Widely as the circumstances differ, the effect and mode of appeal might not inaptly
be compared with an address, such as that of Latimer's at
St Paul's Cross, disseminated through a metropolitan audience
to the length and breadth of Protestant England.

As regards the precise form adopted, classification soon slips
into pedantry. Literature continually falls into new moulds,
corresponding to the circumstances which call it into being.
Just as Epic and Drama, Dialogue or Oratory, were products of
given conditions, so in Church life new types arose answering
to the needs. One after another Epistles, Apocalypses, Gospels
(canonical and apocryphal) were new phenomena, just as in later
days Canons, Bulls, Homilies, Visitation Charges and Addresses
tend each to create their own peculiar *genre*. The Epistle of James

does not fall into exact line with any others, because the circumstances did not recur. The Epistles of Paul were letters, occasional and topical, or else expository and doctrinal: that of James is not strictly a letter. There are no greetings at the opening, or the close: the salutation is formal and impersonal, in the manner of a charge or manifesto. The closest parallel is perhaps that of the First Epistle of Peter; but there the note is both more local and more pastoral. This is a declaration of convictions and principles, somewhat in the manner of prophets of old, addressed to those of his own nation with whom he came into spiritual touch. It is not a set address delivered upon one occasion, nor is it a literary exercise modelled upon the *diatribes*[1] (διατριβαί) of philosophers discoursing with their pupils; but like the Sermon on the Mount it is a compendium of the utterances which from time to time James, at the centre of Jewish Christianity, was wont to address to those who accepted or were prepared to give a sympathetic hearing to the Christian interpretation of Jesus, as fulfilling the Messianic expectation. Gentiles are not excluded, but lie beyond his purview; his own outlook is Jewish, and he does not stray into outlying territory. Whether all was penned by James himself, or by a reporter, is a matter of secondary importance[2]. We cannot particularise the mode of preservation or of publication. The point is—Is it an authentic expression of his personality and outlook? Some sections, particularly in chs. i–iii, are written out at length, with illustrations and turns of speech filled in: others are detached paragraphs; others again hardly more than head-lines ready for expansion in delivery. But all have a physiognomy of their own, and preserve the accent and vocabulary of the teacher, in reproducing the gist of that which was most vital, impressive and permanent in his message.

[1] Ropes pp. 10–18 presses this much further than the conditions allow.
[2] The same is true of Paul, and of authors of every kind, ancient or modern: some write, some dictate, some are taken down. *Paradise Lost* was written by an amanuensis: Gladstone's post-cards most often by himself. Epictetus is known to us through Arrian; but throughout the style and manner of the teacher are almost as patent as in *ipsissima verba*. Autoscript is not the final measure of value.

CHAPTER IV

FORM, STYLE AND COMPOSITION

Before proceeding to the contents of the Epistle, it will be well to grasp the salient features of manner and style. The hand is not that of a skilled or practised writer, with easy command of his resources or his pen. Except in ch. i, and there not without digression and inconsequences, there is no ordered exposition of theme: neither is there sustained copious flow of words, such as we find in St Paul, still less any of the cultured rhetoric and Hellenism that distinguish the Epistle to the Hebrews. Transitions of thought are often abrupt, though it is usually easy to discern the thread, hanging on some verbal connexion; but the movement is discursive and, more and more as the Epistle proceeds, it drops into detached and undeveloped notes of exhortation. The style is short and energetic, with a certain ruggedness resulting from the high moral tension at which the author writes; but there is nothing dictatorial in the address; imperatives do indeed abound (there are over fifty in the five brief chapters)—but they are far more often imperatives of appeal—'*Humble yourselves before the face of the Lord* (iv. 10), '*Suffer long*' (v. 7, 8), '*Be patient therefore*' (v. 7), '*Receive with meekness*' (i. 21), '*Draw near to God*' (iv. 8), '*Hearken, brethren beloved*' (ii. 5)—than imperatives of dictation or reproof. And the phrasing has a force and pungency, which convey the impression of character and conviction, accompanied by gifts of illustration and of racy observation, such as lend charm and physiognomy to Bunyan's prose. In its colloquial turns and interrogations, its dramatic forms of address and second-person appeal[1], the work is clearly that of the preacher rather than the pamphleteer, and of the preacher of the aphoristic and prophetic not the homiletic type, the preacher of few words intensely felt, having the accent 'of authority and not as the

---

[1] ἴδε, ἰδού iii. 3, 4, ἄγε νῦν iv. 13, v. 1, ἀλλ' ἐρεῖ τις ii. 18, and still more the recurrent ἀδελφοί i. 2, 16, 19, ii. 1, 5, 14, iii. 1, 10, 12, iv. 11, v. 7, 9, 10, 12, 19.

scribes.' The adages and maxims introduced, such as '*Slow to speak, slow to wrath*' (i. 19), '*Mercy glorieth against judgment*'[1] (ii. 13), '*Faith without works is dead*' (ii. 26), are not impromptus, but summaries of reflection and experience, familiar probably upon his lips. There is in fact little of quotation[2], beyond the employment of individual words charged with their own O.T. associations. On the other hand there is active literary susceptibility: it is remarkable that five short chapters of exhortation should yield no less than thirteen words for which there is no precedent. χροσοδακτύλιος is a happy accident, worthy of Lucian. But of the verbs, all—except perhaps ἀνεμιζόμενος, 'bewinded' or 'wind-blown,' and the somewhat venturous θρῆσκος for 'an observant'—are well-formed and scholarly; among substantives, ἀποσκίασμα and ῥυπαρία; among adjectives, ἀνέλεος, ἀπείραστος, δαιμονιώδης, well deserve a place in the vocabulary, while how the ancient world carried on without δίψυχος it is hard to imagine; in neatness and in pregnancy μεγαλόψυχος cannot compare with it. In the struggles of Christianity with Hellenism, heathenism and philosophies, it was a valuable addition to the vocabulary, and once invented it was eagerly caught up and exploited by Clement of Rome, Barnabas, the Didache, Hermas and their successors. In *Dipsychus* A. H. Clough pays modern and unexpected tribute to its value. The author seldom falls back on classical diction outside the range of the LXX; but when he does— as in βρύω, εὐπειθής, ἐφήμερος, κατήφεια—his choice is in its kind impeccable.

Throughout the language is steeped in the Scriptural tradition; but habitually in its Greek dress, and largely from the Hellenistic contributors. The Hebrew cast of expression has led some to assume an Aramaic original[3], and then to go a step further by

[1] The absence of connecting particle shows that κατακαυχᾶται ἔλεος κρίσεως is aphoristic.
[2] The proof text on the faith of Abraham from Gen. xv. 6, the familiar summary of the Law from Lev. xix. 18 (as in Mt. xxii. 39), the withering of the grass from Is. xl. 6–7, and the inexact quotation 'love covereth a multitude of sins' practically exhaust the list. It would be hard to find a more glaring contrast than the Epistle of Clement to the Corinthians.
[3] Propounded by J. Wordsworth *Stud. Bibl.* pp. 142 ff.; criticised by

transferring to the translator responsibility for the salutations in
i. 1 and ii. 1. The procedure is arbitrary, without any vestige
of support in tradition; and is decisively negatived by internal
literary evidence. The play on χαίρειν and χαράν—'greeting' and
'joy'—in i. 1 wears the stamp of originality, and is not a translated
play on words: as for an addition prefixed by the redactor, it is
too much to suppose that the address began with 'all joy' (πᾶσαν
χαρὰν ἡγήσασθε) preparing the way inadvertently for the happy
play of the Greek χαίρειν, 'greeting.' Again, in ii. 1 the excision of
the salutation leaves the following clause—'for if there come'—
suspended in the air. The connexion hangs upon the 'not in
respect of persons,' which opens the salutation, and which itself
is not from a translator's hand, but bears the stamp of Palestinian
Christianity[1]. Transitions or sequences of thought effected through
the particular word employed are a characteristic feature of style,
and are evidence that the original medium is preserved. In
i. 3–4 (ὑπομονήν—ὑπομονή) 'patience,' or better 'endurance,' in
v. 4–5 'lacking' and 'lacketh' (λειπόμενοι—λείπεται), in v. 6
'wavering' and 'wavereth' (διακρινόμενος) are instances, which
lose something in the process of translation; but the most conclusive instance is that furnished by the alternation of meanings
in the use of 'tempt' and 'temptation' (πειρασμός—πειράζεσθαι)
which betrays the author into confusion and indeed open in-
consistency of thought. 'Count it all joy,' he begins, 'when ye
fall into manifold *temptations*,' where the word is used in the
established O.T. sense of trials, 'tryings,' probations, disciplines,
administered by God for the perfecting of the cardinal virtues

Zahn i. 118; so Burkitt *Christian Beginnings* p. 69. Bacon *N.T. Introduction* p. 160 dismisses it as 'an example of desperate expedients.'

[1] Jas. ii. 1 μὴ ἐν προσωπολημψίαις ἔχετε τὴν πίστιν τοῦ κυρίου ἡμῶν
Ἰησοῦ Χριστοῦ τῆς δόξης. ἐὰν γὰρ εἰσέλθῃ....Other commentators fasten
on 'the broken clause' (as they deem it) involved by τῆς δόξης, and would
cut the knot by omitting ἡμῶν Ἰησοῦ Χριστοῦ, once more without any
manuscript support. But each proposal introduces new difficulties: no
writer prepared to speak of Christ as 'the Lord of glory' (as in 1 Cor. ii. 8)
would have shrunk from inserting ἡμῶν Ἰησοῦ Χριστοῦ. The reference
to the historic Jesus is, we shall see, essential to the context, and the
titular τῆς δόξης is a genuine and valuable relic of Judaic Christianity
(p. 90–92): προσωπολημψία is emphasised by Hort as illustrating
dialectical variation in Palestinian Greek.

of faith and endurance. The same sense is resumed in *v.* 12 'Blessed is the man that endureth *temptation*,' while in the very next verse he drops into the alternative sense of '*temptations to sin*,' and writes 'Let no man when *tempted* say I am *tempted* of God...,who himself *tempteth* no man.' Clearly the lapse is due to the equivocal use of the *Greek* word.

The numerous verbal echoes from the LXX and the Sapiential books, have not passed through the medium of translation; nor would a translator have hit off the ἅπαξ λεγόμενα found in the Epistle. Throughout, his debt to the LXX is paramount; he seldom if ever seems to have drawn upon the original Hebrew, though that may be due in part to the circumstances of those whom he addresses. Where there is widening of the bounds, it comes from Hellenic culture, and is in the direction of literary appreciation, more than of ethical or psychological precision. ἀμᾶν, βοή, μαραίνειν, ὄψιμος καὶ πρόϊμος, ῥιπίζειν, σήπειν, τρυφᾶν, φρίσσειν, φλογίζειν are instinct with poetic feeling, and add prophetic colour to his admonitions and appeals. His love of assonance and alliteration, his constant parallelism of words, or rhythms, or forms of clause, are all symptoms of his familiarity with Hebrew poetry, and show how much it has directly, or mediately, affected his forms of expression.

Metaphor is a feature of his style—more frequent and vivid than in any other of the Epistles. Its general character is aphoristic —reminding us of the Synoptic teaching of our Lord—enforcing moral truths by similitudes from nature. These are drawn in part from the language of the prophets and of the Wisdom literature (i. 11, iii. 18, iv. 6, v. 2, 5), in part from personal experience. In all the latter, the colouring is genuinely Palestinian, from scenery familiar to St James. Some are from peasant life (iii. 18), like that of the husbandman, long-suffering in expectation of '*the early and the latter rain*' (v. 7). The culture is of the fig, the olive and the vine (iii. 12). Even more local is that of '*the sun rising with the scorching wind*' (i. 11)—τῷ καύσωνι, the Simoon of the Eastern desert—'*and withering the grass*,' worked out in terms adapted from Isaiah, Job and Jonah[1]. Others are maritime, drawn

[1] Mayor, *in loc.*

38   FORM, STYLE AND COMPOSITION

from the Sea of Galilee[1], and vividly impressionist: '*The light spray whisked* (ῥιπιζόμενος) *from the curling wave*' (i. 6) is his picture of instability; and yet more vivid is the presentment in iii. 4—'*Look again at the boats*[2], *big as they are and driven by gusty squalls, yet veered by a tiny blade, as the stroke of the steerer listeth.*' The somewhat cognate ἁλυκόν of bitter water (iii. 12) is specifically drawn from the Dead Sea, lying within sight of Jerusalem, and in the Bible occurs in that connexion only (Num. xxxiv. 3, 12, Deut. iii. 17, etc.). And even the enigmatic '*set on fire by Gehenna*' may be based on a local reference[3].

Thus in its topical aspects and expression the Epistle bewrays the authorship of a Palestinian Jew, at home in all parts of the Hellenistic Scriptures. It would be hard to imagine a production more in keeping with all that we know of the antecedents and career of James, brother of the Lord. One objection that has been advanced needs brief consideration, that the cast of writing is more literary than could be expected of a Galilean. It is an objection which deserves little weight. True, the general complexion of style is literary, rather than colloquial. But it must be remembered that the literary sense can be effectually imparted and transmitted through the oral as well as the written medium. Instances abound from many ages and civilisations, none more telling than that of Greek itself, under its various phases of development—unless indeed we turn to the conservation of Hebrew as the permanent organ of Jewish religion. Among the Jews, education was in universal demand; and everywhere, in school and synagogue, it was based on solid literary footings, partly Hebraic, partly Greek. And the composition of the Epistle, it

[1] With the θαλάσσης of Jas. i. 6, compare ἡ θάλασσα τῆς Γαλιλαίας Mt. iv. 18, viii. 26–32, xiii. 1, xiv. 24, xv. 29 and many parallels in Mark (e.g. i. 16, iv. 1, etc.) and John, showing how ἡ θάλασσα was the habitual term in the vernacular.

[2] τὰ πλοῖα, like θάλασσα, is the habitual word of the shipping on the Sea of Galilee; μετάγειν, for which lexical evidence is curiously scanty (*vide* Hort), was part I suspect of the lake-side vernacular: as may well be true of the recurrent παράγειν (intrans.) in the Gospels; and κλύδωνι is comparatively so uncommon a term, that I should give the same explanation to ἐπετίμησεν τῷ ἀνέμῳ καὶ τῷ κλύδωνι τοῦ ὕδατος.

[3] On this strange verse, a note will be found on p. 59–60.

will be observed, is not that of a student immersed in books, turning up references and verifying his quotations, but that of one steeped in the literary traditions and forms of his spiritual forefathers, and appropriating their language to the needs of his own day. It is time surely to discard the figment of Galilæan illiteracy. It was based upon that piecemeal criticism, which builds upon the minor pedantries and amid the little trees of erudition loses sight of the main wood. Philodemus the philosopher, Meleager the epigrammatist and anthologist, Theodorus the rhetorician, and one may almost add Josephus[1] the historian, were all of Galilee; a little later, Justin Martyr of Samaria. All Christian literature that has survived was written in Greek; it was the chosen medium of Peter, of John, of James, of Jude[2]— of the Gospels, including that according to St Matthew; while the theory of Aramaic originals is little more than ingenious conjecture. It is not sufficiently recognised that the Jews were the most literary of all Mediterranean nations—far more so than the Greeks, or the Romans whose literature was exotic: they gave literary form to their history, their poetry, their religion: they were *par excellence* the people of 'the Books'; in no other nation was there a literary tradition and profession and status such as were accorded to the Scribes. No nation showed readier assimilation and acceptance of the Hellenic culture, installed by Alexander. The LXX marks the Jewish adoption of Hellenism, and it rapidly became the manual of the synagogue and the whole Dispersion west of the Jordan. In our Epistle, while the Hellenistic colouring is marked, it is drawn entirely (except the one baffling phrase τὸν τροχὸν τῆς γενέσεως) from what may be called Scriptural sources[3].

[1] Josephus was born and bred in Jerusalem, but was charged with the administration of Galilee, until its subjugation by Vespasian. The *Jewish War*, his earliest work, he originally composed in Aramaic, but himself translated into Greek, to which he adhered in all his subsequent writings.

[2] In this family connexion it is even worth noting that Clopas—brother, it would seem, to Joseph—had adopted a Greek name (abbreviated from Cleopatros = Cleopas).

[3] In τέλειοι καὶ ὁλόκληροι, the τέλειος is sacrificial rather than Stoic. For study of Hellenistic colour, see H. A. Kennedy in *Expositor*, 8th Series, ii. 37–51.

And—in the way characteristic of acquired speech—the Hellenism shows itself in vocabulary, not in idiom or in the build of sentences. In the use of moods, conjunctions, subordinate sentences, and connecting particles, there is no Greek flexibility[1]; the style remains elementary, and Aramaic in its simplicity.

Before we leave this section of the subject, one point deserves especial notice, the just balance which the writer maintains between the various portions of the sacred books. The Jew divided Scripture into three groups—the Law, the Prophets, and the Other Writings, consisting of Psalms, Odes and the various books of the Wisdom literature.

To the Law (*Torah*) James gives the first place of honour and sanctity. Throughout ch. i the book of Genesis is the authentic revelation of God's creative purpose and intention: *the Law* (ii. 10–13) is the final expression of the moral demands of God, and, as interpreted by Jesus, has become '*the royal law*' '*of liberty*' perfecting the soul's harmony with God (ii. 8, 12, i. 25). Abraham, '*the friend of God*,' is the type of righteousness realised in active and operative faith (ii. 21–25). His debt to *the Prophets* is not so much one of quotation, as of accent, inspiration and mode of appeal. In such a passage as v. 1–6 the voice is the voice of Amos or Isaiah. The largest direct debt is to Isaiah[2], but scattered words and phrases show his assured and intimate familiarity with Hosea, with Jeremiah and with Zechariah.

And lastly no book in N.T. is so deeply impregnated with the later literature of the Jewish moralists, the literature of ethical precept and principle and conduct, the wisdom of Proverbs (v. 20) and of the son of Sirach (i. 12). The '*crown of life*' (i. 12) is indubitably derived from the Hebraic *atarah*[3], which became so

[1] Zahn i. 117 gives details: in the whole Epistle, three sentences only are periodic, and the writer rarely ventures more than one subordinate clause, cf. Maynard Smith p. 15.

[2] For instances, see i. 10–11, 25–7, v. 1–4.

[3] Cf. Abrahams *The Glory of God* p. 70, and *Studies of Pharisaism* p. 169. στέφανος is the habitual LXX equivalent, and has nothing to do with the στέφανος denoting the garland of the victor in the games (as in 1 Cor. ix. 25), which is remote from the atmosphere of James. The Hebraic use, frequently with the descriptive genitive, is familiar to Paul (e.g. 1 Thes. ii. 19, 2 Tim. iv. 8), and James' own expression στέφανος

favourite an image with Rabbinic teachers from Hillel onwards. In their teaching it is woven out of humility and prayer. 'Wisdom' in these pages sounds with a wholly different ring from that which meets us in the pages of St Paul. It is not the speculative wisdom of the Greek, but the moral and practical wisdom of the preacher and the sage: he repeats the ancient adage 'The fear of the Lord that is wisdom, and to depart from evil is understanding'[1] in terms effectively modernised—'*Who is wise and understanding among you? let him show forth by good behaviour his works in meekness of wisdom*' (iii. 13). '*If any of you lack wisdom,*' he begins (i. 5), '*let him ask of God.*' His contrast is between the wisdom of this world, earthly and carnal, and '*the wisdom from above, first pure, then peaceable, gentle, easy to be intreated, full of mercy and good fruits, without variance, without hypocrisy*' (iii. 17). Job is his example of that patience or endurance, to which he gives first place among the cardinal virtues (v. 11). From this aspect it is hardly too fanciful to call his epistle *The Wisdom of James the Just*[1]. And from beginning to end he adheres to the Jewish tradition of preserving and reproducing the aphorisms of the wise men of the past, rather than to the Greek tradition of innovation, discussion and analysis drawn from immediate experience.

τῆς ζωῆς occurs in Rev. ii. 10. It is interesting to note in 1 P. v. 4 the blending of Hebraic and Hellenic phrase in τὸν ἀμαράντινον τῆς δόξης στέφανον.

[1] So Boyd Carpenter.

CHAPTER V

ETHIC

From first to last the mainspring of the Epistle is ethical: the other lines of interest are secondary, and for the most part incidental, arising out of the moral demands and principles enforced, or underlying them as the sanctions on which they ultimately rest. It is an ethic answering to a definite situation, which goes far to determine the emphasis laid upon the sins rebuked and virtues enjoined. In the Epistle of St Peter, or incidentally in the Letters of St Paul, the stress falls chiefly on points of domestic and personal behaviour, on the relations of husbands and wives, masters and servants, friends and familiars, but these are not the province with which James is chiefly concerned. His ethic is more denominational than domestic, dealing with the moral obligations which follow from the Christian rendering of the ancient Law. At the last parting of the ways he saw with prophetic intuition that the choice lay between regeneration founded upon the forbearances of love, and final suicide of the national hopes. '*The fruit of righteousness is sown in peace for them that make peace*' (iii. 18). The last flicker of Jewish independence, or rather self-direction, was realised in the union of the severed provinces or ethnarchies under the undivided sovereignty of Herod Agrippa I (A.D. 41–44). His short-lived sway was signalised by the acts of persecution, the execution[1] of James son of Zebedee and the imprisonment of Peter, which promoted James to the vacant leadership of the Christians of Jerusalem. Within three years the tragedy of his catastrophic death left the throne tenantless, and the government of Palestine reverted to the hands of Roman procurators. The excesses of a Cumanus[2] (A.D. 48–52), a Felix[3] (A.D. 52–59) or a Festus (A.D. 60–

[1] The kingly power included the life and death prerogative, which had never been entrusted to the Sanhedrim.
[2] Jos. *B. J.* II. xii. See later p. 112.
[3] See p. 112. Jos. *B. J.* II. xiii, Tac. *Hist.* v. 9.

62) may have hastened the throes of dissolution, but the virus of disintegration lay in the internecine jealousies of fanatical and irreconcileable sects, which found typical expression in the Zealots, the Sicarii, and the false Messiahs[1], and which terrorised capital and country alike with wholesale rapine, fire and blood. At this crisis in their history, the Jews, abandoning that trust in a guiding and directive providence, which through centuries had been

> The fountain light of all their day,
> The master light of all their seeing,

took their destinies into their own hands, and, defiant of the demands and restraints of righteousness, discarding all dictates of humanity, of good faith and of all godly fear, challenged the supremacy of Rome and in a welter of anarchy and civil wars rushed the nation to its doom.

'*Blessed the man who endureth*' is the text of his discourse: and it is no wonder that James gives the foremost place in his appeal to that patience, or rather endurance[2], which had been the saving characteristic of the chosen people. '*The proof of your faith worketh endurance: let endurance have its perfect work, that ye may be perfect and entire, in nothing falling short*' (i. 3, 4). The endurance of which he speaks is not the self-sufficing determination of Stoic will, which defies outward circumstance: nor is it the self-imposed renunciation of the ascetic, still less the cringing submission of the slave. It is the characteristic resignation of the Jew, unparalleled in history, which combines immoveable tenacity of purpose with obedient compliance to constraint of circumstance and *force majeure*. It is essentially Hebraic, not developed from within but reposing on assured belief in a higher power, or '*faith*'—which in St James as in the Epistle to the Hebrews means always 'trust' in God—an invincible assurance 'that he is, and is a rewarder of them that seek him out' (Heb. xi. 6).

---

[1] Jos. *B. J.* II. xiii. See p. 49 n. for references.

[2] ὑπομονή is one of the words which belong almost entirely to the later books of the LXX. In the Maccabæan period (esp. 4 Macc.) it assumes its place of honour among the virtues; and the contrast between it and Stoic ἀνδρεία, καρτερία, θάρσος, etc., is instructive. In the Gospels, Luke (viii. 15, xxi. 19) twice puts it in the mouth of Jesus, and there is no other use.

44 ETHIC

The dramatised type is in Job—'*Ye have heard of the patience of Job*' (v. 11) culminating in the utterance, 'Though he slay me, yet will I trust in him,'[1] justified in the issue, the final result, in which (says James) '*ye have seen the end of the Lord, that the Lord is full of pity and merciful.*' Such endurance then is not so much a quality or innate disposition of soul, as an attained condition, the resultant of faith tempered, steeled as we may say, and put to proof. In an unusual phrase, quoted by Peter and paralleled in Paul, it is described as that ingredient in faith which has been 'put to the test' and has emerged refined and purged. It is the constancy—in the words of the Collect[2] the 'constancy of our faith even unto death'—which has been subject to the disciplines of 'trying' or 'temptation,' the temper of the seasoned veteran, which only through the ordeals of hardship and struggle can attain to full development. '*The proof of your faith worketh endurance*[3]: *but let endurance have its perfect work, that ye may be perfect and entire*' (ὁλόκληροι, free from flaws, faults and blemishes) '*lacking in nothing,*' that is to say, fully developed Christians. The thought, and with it the wording, reminds us of sayings in the Gospels: 'In your endurance ye shall win your souls' (L. xxi. 19), and in the Sermon on the Mount 'Ye then shall be perfect, as your heavenly father is perfect' (Mt. v. 48). Constancy of this kind, advancing through trial to perfection implies a stedfastness of soul, a single-heartedness of aim, which James tellingly contrasts with that of the '*double-minded man*' (i. 8, iv. 8) '*unstable in all his ways.*' Trial, then, endurance and trust are the key-note of his message; but they must take effect in act, without which they lose all vitality. Evidently he belongs to a society, in which there was a danger of religious profession drowning, and by

[1] Job xiii. 15.   [2] Collect for Innocents' Day.
[3] i. 3–4 τὸ δοκίμιον ὑμῶν τῆς πίστεως κατεργάζεται ὑπομονήν. The suggestion for the phrase came perhaps from 4 Macc. xvii. 12, where of the seven martyred sons it is written, 'In that divine conflict virtue putting them to proof by endurance (ἀρετὴ δι' ὑπομονῆς δοκιμάζουσα) set before them the prize of victory in incorruption in life everlasting.' This may well have supplied the suggestion, but is not enough to account for the parallelism. The arresting form given to it by James is echoed in Rom. v. 3–4 ἡ θλίψις ὑπομονὴν κατεργάζεται ἡ δὲ ὑπομονὴ δοκιμήν, and virtually quoted in 1 Pet. i. 7. The problem of literary associations is treated later pp. 84 and 96.

degrees asphyxiating religious practice. What were the appointed 'trials' or disciplines by which the Christian graces were to be 'breathed and exercised'? The contrast between the Pauline Epistles and our own is glaring. Among the lists of evil-doing furnished by St Paul, let us take that, which in time and place falls nearest to our own[1]. 'Fornication, uncleanness, lasciviousness, idolatry, sorcery, enmities, strife, jealousies, wraths, factions, divisions, heresies, envyings, drunkenness, revellings and such like.' Here are whole classes of sins, which do not figure in this Epistle: they are native to the heathen life of cities, in which idolatry and superstition, lust and debauchery, self-indulgence, quarrelling and greed ran riot. Of this there is nothing in James: he moves in another atmosphere, which obviously represents the *milieu* familiar to himself[2]. He is not a systematic moralist, classifying, analysing and appraising the various kinds of virtue and vice; rather he is discursive, often reiterative, and impetuous in his affirmation of certain axioms of right conduct and belief. He is no casuist, inventing and resolving cases of conscience, but at every turn a realist, drawing from direct experience—'*If there come into synagogue a man with a gold ring*' (ii. 2), '*Do they not hale you into court?*' (ii. 6), '*Look too at the boats...*' (iii. 4), *Whence wars and whence battles?...*' (iv. 1),'*Go to now, ye rich...*' (v. 1). Turns like this carry their own guarantee of actuality, and assure us that he is holding up the mirror to what was going on around him. '*Where jealousy and faction is, there is confusion and all manner of villainy*' (iii. 16). Moral unsettlement and instability[3] was a note of the social and religious environment. Of organised persecution[4], political or ecclesiastical, the epistle gives no evidence, nor even of violence arising out of differences of

[1] Gal. v. 19–20. For a similar catalogue, even more Gentile in complexion, see Rom. i. 28–32, and for other parallels, Jewish and Christian, Knox *St Paul and the Church of Jerusalem* p. 23, n. 49.

[2] 'Only as an expression of the attitude of the primitive Church in Jerusalem, does the Epistle of St James become intelligible.' Knox *St Paul and the Church of Jerusalem* p. 21, n. 44.

[3] ἀκαταστασία iii. 16, i. 8. The same word occurs in 1 Cor. xiv. 33 as the antithesis of 'peace,' in the conduct of public worship.

[4] v. 6 κατεδικάσατε, ἐφονεύσατε will be discussed later; the reference is to forms of judicial murder, committed by individuals through processes of law.

observance, Jewish, Gentile or heathen. The hardships[1], the indignities, the trials (i. 2) his readers have to face, are such as fall to the lot of the down-trodden and obscure; resulting from distinctions of class and position (ii. 1–6), from social prejudice and greed, from pride of place, from religious rancour and disdain. Special stress is laid on the misuse and abuse of wealth (ii. 1–6, iv. 13–16), on the vanity of riches (iv. 13–14), and on the exactions of the profiteer (v. 1–4). Phrases of ancient prophecy intensify the writer's note, as he voices the cry of those into whose soul the iron is entering, as the champion of the victimised and the oppressed. But even so he will allow no compromise; no extremity of provocation can invalidate the law of love; its mandate knows no limit, and even under the extreme ordeal '*You have sentenced, you have done to death the just*' (v. 6), the tenet of non-resistance still holds—'*He doth not resist you*' is for the Christian an inviolable law, and the gospel of endurance passes into the gospel of long-suffering[2]. His most vehement protest leads to the conclusion '*Be ye therefore long-suffering*' (v. 7). Until this tyranny be overpast, two consolations uphold the fortitude of the believer; first that great reversal of judgments, in which at a higher bar the temporary miscarriages of this world's verdicts will be rectified (v. 8–9), and secondly, the imminence of that reversal—'*Lo, the judge standeth before the doors,*' '*Be ye long-suffering, until the appearing of the Lord*' (v. 7), '*The appearing of the Lord is at hand*' (v. 8). As in the first days, as in the earlier Epistles of Paul[3], as in Peter, and even in the Epistle to the Hebrews the expectation of 'the day,' 'the coming of the Lord' is still a spring of vital power.

[1] κακοπαθεία v. 10, 13.

[2] For μακροθυμεῖν, μακροθυμία there is little place in classical morality. It is man's reproduction of the divine forbearance (Ex. xxxiv. 6, Rom. ii. 4, ix. 22), the opposite of the spirit of retaliation (Col. i. 11 with Lightfoot's note). From the side of the superior, it appears in Proverbs 'He that is slow to anger is better than the mighty' (xvi. 32; cf. xix. 11); but in Christian ethics, from the side of the inferior it finds wider scope.

[3] Above all in the Epistles to the Thessalonians, where the expectation of the Coming stands in the forefront of the argument, and of the Apostolic warnings. In the later Pauline groups it passes more and more into the background: but for its active influence in Jewish Christianity see 1 P. iv. 7, 13, Heb. x. 25.

Beside patience and long-suffering he sets the companion grace of Humility (i. 9, 10, iv. 6, 10), a virtue characteristic of Jewish in contrast with Pagan morality[1]. It only attains spiritual value as the standard of comparison is transferred from man to God. To the Greek and Roman, comparing man with man, it implied some want of self-respect: to the Jew it measured man's littleness compared with the unapproachable holiness of God; and in N.T. the lineage remains unmistakeable: James and Peter (1 P. v. 5) agree in quoting Prov. iii. 3, '*he giveth grace to the humble,*' as the proof text. In the teaching of Jesus[2] it receives new consecrations, which have left their impress on the writings both of Peter and Paul, but there is no certain trace of these in our Epistle. '*Humble yourselves in the sight of the Lord, and he shall exalt you*' (iv. 10) finds an exact parallelism in L. xiv. 11, but both may rest upon O.T. antecedents. Here as throughout he is the practical moralist; he does not attempt analysis, but he realises its intrinsic worth when he presses it upon Jew and Christian alike, upon the well-to-do and the brother of low degree (i. 9), upon the sinner and the sinned against. The test might come from different sides, but only in reverent self-effacements before God could unity of soul be gained—'*Draw nigh to God, and he will draw nigh to you: cleanse your hands, ye sinners, and make pure your hearts, ye double-minded*' (iv. 8). In such appeal James rises to his height.

But there is one particular department of evil—sins of the tongue—which is nowhere else singled out for rebuke with the same passion of energy and conviction. '*The tongue can no man tame; it is a disordering evil, full of deathly poison*' (iii. 8); '*it constitutes the order of unrighteousness among our members*' (iii. 6).

[1] For its primacy in the Rabbinic scale of virtues see Montefiore *Old Testament and After* p. 439.
[2] In the recurrent ὁ ὑψῶν ἑαυτὸν ταπεινωθήσεται of L. xiv. 11, xviii. 14 (and cf. i. 52), Mt. xxiii. 12, Jesus crystallises the antithesis already established in the language of Isaiah and the Psalms. The ταπεινοφροσύνην ἐγκομβώσασθε of 1 P. v. 5 reads like personal reminiscence of the Upper Chamber. The great saying πραΰς εἰμι καὶ ταπεινὸς τῇ καρδίᾳ (Mt. xi. 29) underlies 2 Cor. x. 1, Eph. iv. 2 and Col. iii. 12, and it is noticeable how ταπεινός and ταπεινοῦν are associated by Paul with the self-humiliation of Christ (2 Cor. x. 1, Phil. ii. 8).

Already in ch. i it has been on the tip of his tongue—'*If any man deemeth himself religious*'[1]—an observant of religion (θρῆσκος) —'*and bridleth not his tongue..., that man's observance is vain*' (i. 26): and it recurs with the same reference in iv. 11, 16. Parallels of a kind may be found in Proverbs, warnings directed against foolish, vain and irresponsible talking—e.g. 'the lips of the fool that are without understanding'; but the language of James shows no trace of verbal borrowing, it is the writer's own, the outcome not of books, but of experience. Nor is filthy and unseemly talk in question, as in Eph. v. 4 and elsewhere, nor again except subordinately the malicious and backbiting tongues of Rom. i. 29, iii. 13, Eph. iv. 25, 31, etc. Read with care, the chapter shows clear and unmistakeable intention: the sins of the tongue assailed are those of religious faction. The chapter opens with the words '*Be not many teachers*,' not 'a mob of disputants' clamouring for self-assertion. He is writing to a society rent with schisms, torn with religious factions, with '*bitterness and mutual spite*,'[2] whose very existence was threatened by intestine feuds and controversies, '*by spiritual boasting, lying against the truth*.'[3] No proficiency in learning could atone for the moral insensibility which would be the undoing of religion and society[4]. We are reminded of the conditions antecedent to the Corcyræan massacres in the pages of Thucydides, and never were they more fatally reproduced than in the Jerusalem of A.D. 50–70. "Under cover of specious watchwords the rival leaders exploited the interests they professed to serve, and in reckless competition for ascendancy perpetrated the most horrible outrages followed by reprisals still more shocking, glutting the passions of the hour at the bidding of partisan caprice. Frantic violence was the test of manliness; the extremist alone commanded confidence, and all protest was suspect."[5] The strife of tongues was the cancer at the heart of Israel. All sense of national unity, all reverence for authority, all patient waiting upon God were

---

[1] E.V. 'religious' and 'religion' are by themselves misleading; the terms refer to outward religion, much like the medieval use of 'the religious' as contrasted with the laity. The sense of observance is prominent in A. xxvi. 5, and Col. ii. 18, the only other occasions of N.T. use.

[2] ζῆλον πικρὸν καὶ ἐριθείαν iii. 14, on which see p. 114 n.

[3] μὴ κατακαυχᾶσθε καὶ ψεύδεσθε κατὰ τῆς ἀληθείας iii. 14.

[4] iii. 16 ἐκεῖ ἀκαταστασία καὶ πᾶν φαῦλον πρᾶγμα.   [5] Thuc. III. 82.

being drowned in a Babel of conflicting cries. The traditional
and more stable combinations—Pharisee, Sadducee, or Essene—
were dissolving into groups of reckless and unbridled partisans.
At Jerusalem social feuds, political or ecclesiastical intrigue,
personal ambitions, all donned the mask of religion, and in its
name proceeded to acclaim their own prophet, to frame their own
shibboleths, and to imprecate anathemas on all opponents[1]. In the
provinces[2]—in Judæa, Samaria, Galilee, and beyond Jordan—each
ringleader of sedition with the cry Lo here! Lo there! proclaimed
himself prophet or 'Christ.' For a parallel to the state of affairs
depicted in Josephus, we might turn to the sixteenth-century
wars of religion in Germany, or to the ceaseless wrangles of
sectaries, which compassed the fall of the English Commonwealth,
and set the match[3] to the constitutional framework, on which
all national liberties depended. In this respect at least the atmosphere in which James moved was like that which led Milton[4]
to write of 'the noise of flocking birds...who in their envious
gabble prognosticate a year of sects and schisms.' The spirit of
controversy was a deadly bane, the offspring of spiritual rebellious-
ness and pride. It might claim high-sounding credentials of
'wisdom' and 'understanding' (iii. 13), but in truth it was the
contradiction of the true and 'heavenly wisdom' (iii. 15). And
in the epithets attached to it, rendered '*earthly, sensual, devilish,*'
we note again a genuinely Palestinian touch in the word '*de-
moniacal.*'[5] Nowhere else would the new coinage be so natural

[1] This explains the special point of iii. 8–9: ἀκατάστατον κακόν, μεστὴ
ἰοῦ θανατηφόρου. ἐν αὐτῇ εὐλογοῦμεν τὸν κύριον καὶ πατέρα, καὶ ἐν αὐτῇ
καταρώμεθα τοὺς ἀνθρώπους. 'Death-dealing venom' becomes an appropriate metaphor, and the unusual τὸν κύριον καὶ πατέρα may well rest
on some topical reference, or party shibboleth.

[2] For risings of Theudas, A. v. 36; and—under Fadus—in Jos. *Ant.*
xx. v; for Judas the Galilean, A. v. 37, Jos. *Ant.* XVIII. i. 1, *B. J.* II. viii. 1,
with which compare *Ant.* xx. i. 1, viii. 6 and *B. J.* II. xii. 4, II. xiii. See
p. 112. Historic instances are later; but ψευδόχριστοι of Mk. xiii, 22,
Mt. xxiv. 24 are valid proof.

[3] On φλογίζουσα, see *Note* appended to this chapter.

[4] *Areopagitica*, p. 72.

[5] ἐπίγειος, ψυχική, δαιμονιώδης—the latter found only in Scholia
to Aristophanes, and in a later version of the LXX, which came from the
hand of a Samaritan [Symmachus, later half of second century]. For

as in the land where claims to spiritual insight and authority were familiarly ascribed to the instigation of 'demons.' 'John came neither eating nor drinking and they say He hath a devil,' and the same charge was levelled at Jesus himself in Jerusalem. Here the adjectives characterise the sordid ambitions and the untamed passions, which led to excesses and pretensions as of men possessed.

Of the duty laid upon Christians under such conditions James speaks with no uncertain voice. '*Be not many teachers my brethren*'[1]; to enter the lists of controversy is to call down '*greater judgment*' upon one's own head. In the organisation of the synagogue, warnings against the vice of religious contentiousness were as needful for Christians as for others. There lay the test of moral sincerity. 'He that refraineth his lips is wise' had been the counsel of Solomon; and 'to keep silence even from good words' was the call laid upon the Christian. It is important to remember this, when we come to consider the writer's own reticences and omissions[2]. To him the one antidote lay in a return to the spirit of meekness realised in *generous behaviour*[3], and engendered by '*the wisdom that is from above*' (iii. 17). The appeal is in striking contrast with that·Greek thought of Wisdom with which the Pauline Epistles familiarise us. This '*Wisdom from above*' is not of the intellectual, but of the moral and 'luminous' type portrayed in the books of Wisdom. In them, as an attempted synthesis of Hebraic and Hellenic thought in their contemplation of the divine, there emerge the semi-personal form and attributes of Wisdom, as the thoughts and utterance of God. This is the '*Wisdom from above*' which James invokes not with direct quotation, but in language permeated with that conception of 'the understanding spirit...unhindered, beneficent, humane' which is distinctive of

δαιμόνιον ἔχει of John the Baptist cf. Mt. xi. 18, L. vii. 33; of Jesus, at Jerusalem, J. vii. 20, viii. 48, 52. There are other parallels, as in Mt. xii. 24–7, Mk. iii. 22, L. xi. 15, 'He casteth out devils by Beelzebub,' and in the accounts of the Temptation.

[1] Jas. iii. 1. The injunction is in strict line with the teaching of Jesus, Mt. xxiii. 2–3 'The Scribes and the Pharisees sit on the seat of Moses: all things therefore whatsoever they say unto you do and observe'— though there is no reference here to the particular *dictum* or occasion.

[2] *Infra* pp. 66–7, 88, 121, 124–6.

[3] ἐκ τῆς καλῆς ἀναστροφῆς τὰ ἔργα ἐν πραΰτητι σοφίας iii. 13.

this school of thought. In James it is even more explicitly moralised and applied to the social conditions round about him; the epithets become even more personal in tone, and touched with those feminine attributes which naturally attached themselves to the ideal *Sophia*. '*The wisdom that is from above is first pure, then making for peace, conciliatory, persuasive, full of mercy and good fruits, single-minded and without hypocrisy.*'[1] Such a sentence declares its origin, and could have proceeded only from one school of thought. In his cry for peace the accent of James reminds us of the attitude ascribed to Lord Falkland before the outbreak of the Civil War. 'When there was any overture or hope of peace, he would be more erecte and rigorous and exceedingly sollicitous to presse any thinge which he thought might promote it, and often after a deep silence...would with a shrill and sadd accent ingeminate the word *Peace Peace*, and would passyonately professe that the very agony of the warr, and the view of the calamityes and desolation the kingdome did and must indure,... would shortly break his heart.' The premonition of the patriot and the prophet is informed with the spirit of Christ, and is expressed in terms which read like direct, though independent, echoes of the teaching of Jesus[2]. And, in literary manner, the close of the chapter presents an interesting parallel to that already

[1] iii. 17 ἁγνή is the more feminine counterpart of the καθαρότης of Wisd. vii. 24; εἰρηνική finds a close parallel in the καρπὸν εἰρηνικὸν δικαιοσύνης of Heb. xii. 11, which is possibly modelled on this passage; ἐπιεικής, εὐπειθής and above all μεστὴ ἐλέους καὶ καρπῶν ἀγαθῶν are strongly personal in cast, and the ἀνυπόκριτος has no LXX precedent except Wisd. v. 18, xviii. 16.

[2] The verbal correspondences are very numerous. In iii. 12 the vine, fig and olive similitude is exactly in the manner (though not the precise words) of Mt. vii. 16–20, and is reinforced by the καρπῶν ἀγαθῶν and καρπὺς τῆς δικαιοσύνης of iii. 17–18. In iii. 13 ἐν πραΰτητι recalls the πραΰς καὶ ταπεινός already dealt with, and the διὰ τῆς πραΰτητος καὶ ἐπιεικείας τοῦ Χριστοῦ (2 Cor. x. 1) agrees with the ἐπιεικής of iii. 17. ἀνυπόκριτος (iii. 17) does indeed occur in Wisdom, but is more probably derived from Gospel teaching (cf. 1 P. i. 22); while τοῖς ποιοῦσιν εἰρήνην (iii. 18) is an exact reproduction of εἰρηνοποιοί of the beatitude (Mt. v. 9). These correspondences show the source from which they proceed, and already ethically, though not yet in the theological and quasi-personal form which was so soon to become current, Jesus is identified by James with '*the Wisdom that is from above.*'

noticed in v. 7. Just as there the denunciation of wealth passes
to the abrupt conclusion '*Be ye therefore long-suffering*,' so here
the passionate appeal for peace passes into the equally abrupt
'*Whence wars and whence battles among you?*' leading on to the
words of warning and of exhortation which fill the two remaining
chapters.

As he finally turns from the subject he reverts in a last word
to that specific and besetting form of evil-speaking, which vents
itself in sectarian strife; religious prejudice and rancour, there
lay the enemy, and as the one hope of cure he appeals to that
bond of brotherhood[1] which rested on yet deeper foundations;
and in so doing goes more to the root of his moral axioms than
in any other passage. If it was in the name of Law that the bond
of brotherhood was so often violated and set at naught, in the
name of Law he pleads for its restoration. '*Talk not one against
the other, brethren*' (how emphatic is the word of address!); '*he
that talketh against a brother, or that judgeth his brother, talketh
against law and judgeth law.*'[2] James is not here referring to special
injunctions of Torah, but to that underlying principle which
governs and comprehends them all, which he has already described
as '*sovereign law*,' the law of freedom and of love. Its mandates
are absolute; he who violates them contravenes the authority and
ruling of Law itself, with its twin rule of love to God and love
to neighbour[3]. He sets himself up as '*law-giver*' and '*judge*'—in
Jewish thought the vice-gerents of God on earth—instead of
accepting the decree of the one supreme '*law-giver and judge*[4]
who has power to save and to destroy.*'

---

[1] Christian categories gave new values to the term 'brother,' perhaps
under the direct initiative of Jesus, as evidenced in the Sermon on the
Mount. From the very first (A. i. 15, 16), and alike in Peter, Paul and
John, it designates the Christian tie, but James played his part in estab-
lishing its place in the currency. For references, see p. 34.

[2] In his use of Law there is something of the same equivocacy that
so often meets us in St Paul, and intrudes indeed into Christ's own
treatment of 'the Law.'

[3] Mk. xii. 29–31 and parallels, echoed in v. 12.

[4] In iv. 12. Just as νομοθέτης thinks of Jehovah, as author of Mosaic
Law, so κριτής clearly thinks of Christ, if we compare (in its context)
'*the judge standeth before the doors*' v. 9.

At this point the Epistle becomes hortative and categorical: such unity as it retains belongs rather to character and feeling, than to studied order in the arrangement, or completeness in exposition. It is in close accord with what we know of personality, an expression of the beliefs and convictions for which James gave his life, his message of salvation to all who would give ear. The sins which he arraigns, the duties which he most emphasises are as it were the headlines upon which his preaching and living were a commentary and expansion, applications of the law of love to phases of the life of trial.

The most developed is the arraignment of misused wealth, with which chap. v opens. It is general in terms, directed against all abuse of wealth, without reference to particular sect or following; and couched largely upon the precedents of O.T. prophets, especially those of Jerusalem—Amos, Isaiah, Habakkuk and Jeremiah. But the charges take their colour from the usurious greed of the high-priestly aristocracy, who controlled the national finance, and through Temple monopolies, and manipulation of the Tribute shekel and rack-renting, amassed fortunes at the expense of the pilgrim hosts who thronged to the great festivals. This backbone of the Jewish Treasury was ruthlessly and ostentatiously[1] exploited by the Sadducean coterie, above all the Annas family, who through the machinery of the Sanhedrin could make processes of law[2] the instrument of their own greed. This prostitution of religion and of law to the ends of personal avarice was a bitter grievance to the poorer classes of the community, and an affront to the moral sense of all God-fearing Jews, and not least to those who resorted to the festivals and were its immediate victims[3]. The scathing indignation of the text becomes

---

[1] Jas. v. 5 ἐτρυφήσατε ἐπὶ τῆς γῆς καὶ ἐσπαταλήσατε. Hort *Ep. James* pp. 107–9 devotes an Appendix to the usage of the word; but the pertinent historical comment may be read in the pages of Josephus.

[2] v. 6 κατεδικάσατε, ἐφονεύσατε τὸν δίκαιον. The severity of the Sadducees in dealing with offenders was notorious (Jos. *Ant.* XIII. x. 6). The process instituted against James himself by Annas is a palmary instance (Jos. *Ant.* XX. ix. 1).

[3] The exactions of the Papal treasury, through claims to patronage, annates, Peter's pence, etc. and later through the sale of indulgences, furnish a not unapt parallel from medieval times

intelligible against this background: the protest would have carried the sympathy of multitudes, but would not be lightly forgotten or forgiven by those directly implicated.

A special interest attaches to the prohibition of oaths enjoined in v. 12. It stands in no obvious connexion with what precedes or what follows, and the overcharged '*Before all*' (πρὸ πάντων) which introduces it, suggests some other context. Nor is the purport of the injunction made quite clear, whether aimed at profane and irreverent speech—as Lev. xxiv. 15–16, Ecclus. xxiii. 9–11—or rather, as the latter half of the verse suggests, at violence and over-emphasis in speech, which dishonours the sacredness of unadorned and simple truth[1]: this was the ground on which the Essenes forbade all oaths in ordinary intercourse; though elaborate and solemn oaths were imposed upon entrants and novices, when admitted to the society[2]. James' own asceticism had points of contact with Essene disciplines, but whether that is the case here or not, the form of oath '*Neither by heaven, nor by earth*' is unmistakeably Judaic and Rabbinic[3], and one more mark of distinctively Palestinian colouring. In a Pauline or Johannine epistle the verse would be out of its element.

The remaining injunctions are concerned with those sides of Christian obligation which naturally found most place in his public preaching. They deal with Christian profession and observance in their public and social contacts, rather than with the life of inner experience, or with the private and domestic relations. Here and there phrases such as '*O adulteresses*' (iv. 4), '*Weep and howl*' (v. 1), '*the ears of the Lord of Sabaoth*' (v. 4),

[1] Mayor collects parallels from Philo, and from other writers—Pagan and Christian.

[2] Jos. *B. J.* II. viii. 5–6 supplies a full and interesting account—and the Quakers, e.g. George Fox *Journal* 224, 255, 328, etc., and Tolstoi yield instructive parallels. The Epistle of Peter prefixed to the *Clementine Homilies* represents James as forbidding swearing as unlawful, but in the same breath dictating to his elders the most solemn oaths of obedience by heaven, earth, water and air. It is just possible that this is a reference to the Epistle, but there is little or nothing to support it.

[3] Philo *Spec. Legg.* M. ii, p. 271. The variations in form found in Clem. Alex., *Clem. Hom.*, Epiphanius and others, point back to an Aramaic original. See Mayor *in loc.*, and for the relation to Mt. v. 34–7, see p. 67–8.

assume prophetic licence, and may be regarded as reproducing a characteristic accent. The besetting sins on which he fastens are those of the society in which he lived, but the selection is influenced by his own outlook upon life. In the denunciations of covetousness (iv. 2), of the pursuit of pleasure (iv. 3, v. 5), of wealth (iv. 13–16, v. 1–4), of worldly ends and aims (v. 13–17), we hear the voice of the ascetic; the call to patience and long-suffering (v. 7–11), and the prohibition of all evil-speaking (iv. 11–12) come from the pacifist; while the positive injunctions are characteristically those of the 'holy man' and devotee. Life is an austere self-dedication, a constant practice of the presence and the fear of God, realised above all in prayer and witness. '*Is any in affliction? let him pray. Is any cheerful? let him sing praise*' (v. 13). In daily act and exercise the life of James bore witness to the place of prayer[1] in the life of consecration. The Epistle from its first precept, '*Let him ask of God who giveth*' (i. 5), to this closing paragraph reflects the spirit of the son of Sirach, 'Be not faint-hearted in thy prayer' (vii. 10), nowhere more closely than in the illustration inspired by 'My son, in thy sickness be not negligent; but pray unto the Lord and he shall heal thee' (xxxviii. 9). But the words used are the writer's own, drawn from his own life, unless indeed he borrows from the oral tradition in which the *Logia* of Jesus were handed down[2]. For efficacious prayer (v. 16), as in the teaching and parables of Jesus, persistence is as vital as earnestness. By a strange freak

[1] See p. 21. Rabbinic insistence upon prayer is well illustrated by Montefiore *Old Testament and After* p. 349 ff., and in his Second Series of *Studies of Pharisaism* Abrahams devotes striking sections (XI and XII) to 'Rabbinic Ideas on Prayer,' and 'The Lord's Prayer.' At p. 76 he refers to the original of Ecclus. vii. 10, and notes how 'Be not faint-hearted' has displaced 'Be not impatient' of the original Hebrew version.

[2] αἰτεῖτε καὶ οὐ λαμβάνετε (iv. 3) is a close verbal parallel to Mt. vii. 7, L. xi. 9 αἰτεῖτε καὶ δοθήσεται, and J. xvi. 4 αἰτεῖτε καὶ λήψεσθε. The μηδὲν διακρινόμενος (i. 6) represents the ἐν καρδίᾳ δισσῇ, 'draw not nigh with a double heart,' of Ecclus. i. 28, but finds its closest verbal parallel in Mt. xxi. 21 ∥ Mk. xi. 23 ἐὰν ἔχητε πίστιν καὶ μὴ διακριθῆτε. This use of the word elucidates the ἀδιάκριτος of iii. 17. The metaphor from the wind-driven spray (i. 6) may well have been suggested by Ecclus. xxxiii. 2 'He that is a hypocrite is as a ship in a squall' (ὡς ἐν καταιγίδι πλοῖον).

of exegesis the two incidental and companion illustrations have been raised to the status of ecclesiastical ordinances, and been made the basis of the Sacraments of *Extreme Unction*, and of auricular *Confession*[1]. The 'anointing with oil' (v. 14) was an established Jewish practice[2]; remedial in origin and intention, it was reinforced (as were almost all prescriptions) with devotional accompaniments, and was 'a sacrament' of healing and recovery, not of preparation for death: its administration by 'elders' gained a permanent place in the usage of the synagogue. Similarly, owing to the association of physical maladies with sins committed or inherited[3], the identification and acknowledgement of sins was regarded as necessary for remission and cure. Illustrations such as these provide no materials for solid argument, and it is not even clear whether they are derived from Jewish practice, or from Christian, or (as seems likely) from both; in which case '*the elders of the congregation*'[4] may well be employed as a deliberately neutral phrase, designed to cover a wide field of address. So far as organisation goes, the synagogue model is still assumed, but that does not preclude incipient stages of institutional Christianity.

The ethic thus presented moves, it must be admitted, within a limited circumference. It is at the core Hebraic, and even we may say Palestinian in scope. It is addressed to a society in which religious rancour and controversy were perhaps the most desolating evils, in which God-fearing profession tended to supplant God-fearing action, and in which sordid and avaricious ends threatened the eclipse and extirpation of spiritual ideals; it assumes a state of things in which these evils could only be countered by the passive virtues of endurance, resignation and long-suffering, and in which relief of the indigent and helpless was a primary province

---

[1] So in the Canons and Anathemas of the Council of Trent. Mayor *in loc.* gives a digest of authorities.

[2] Cf. Mk. vi. 13, L. x. 34. For the use of oil, saliva, and other forms of application in modern faith-healing, and psycho-therapy, Micklem gives a useful survey in *Miracles and the New Psychology*. Mayor and other Commentaries supply full references.

[3] Cf. Mt. ix. 2–5, Mk. ii. 1–12, J. v. 14 and ix. 2, etc.—and the Jewish saying 'No man recovers from sickness, till his sins have been forgiven.' Mayor *in loc.*

[4] v. 14 τοὺς πρεσβυτέρους τῆς ἐκκλησίας.

of Christian loving-kindness. To positive reconstruction[1]—to freer and fuller developments of family life and of civic obligations and activities, to the cardinal vices and shortcomings of heathenism, to the regeneration of the more varied and versatile civilisation and of the intellectual products of Hellenism, to problems of ecclesiastical unity and organisation, to the equipment and adaptation of Christianity as a world-religion—there is no new contribution; the whole atmosphere—social, intellectual and moral —is far more confined than that of the Epistles to Corinth, to Rome, to Ephesus or the Pastorals. But within its own radius there is fine sincerity, consistency, restraint and fearlessness of aim and utterance. He was single-hearted in devotion to his creed; he acted up to his own condemnation of the '*double-minded man, unstable in all his ways*' (i. 8). He naturalised[2] that word among the Christian, or rather the un-Christian, categories of behaviour. For him ancestral 'trust in God' took shape in faithful allegiance to the precepts of '*the Lord Jesus Christ*'; and for fidelity to that conviction he was ready with the Stoic 'to endure and to refrain,'[3] with St Paul 'to spend and to be spent'[4] for the winning of souls, and in the last issue not afraid 'to crown' the dedicated life by the martyr's death (i. 12). 'When the eye is single, the whole body is full of light' (L. xi. 34).

While the material remains Hebraic, texture and colouring become unmistakeably Christian. In truth, no other book in the Bible keeps so close to the actual utterances of Jesus. It is no question of formal salutations (i. 1, ii. 1) or of titular designations 'Christ' and 'Lord' accorded: nor even of oral reminiscences and reproductions, but of a spirit, a new law of liberty, which permeates the whole. By omission, as well as by assertion, the Epistle is a revaluation of Judaism in terms of the thought and teaching of Jesus. The restrictive categories of Judaism—those for instance concerned with descent, with circumcision, with compliance with the Law—are nowhere assailed or slighted, but by silence they

---

[1] As a comment on the deficiencies here noted, see Lock *Paul the Master-Builder* pp. 106–24.

[2] In Clem. Rom., Barnabas, *Didache*, Hermas, adjective, noun and verb have all passed into the Christian currency.

[3] ἀνέχεσθαι καὶ ἀπέχεσθαι. [4] 2 Cor. xii. 15, cf. Jas. v. 20.

are relegated to a secondary place. Jesus becomes the fountain of authority, and the final court of appeal; in him 'faith' is transmuted into new spiritual sensibilities (ii. 1); his word and person constitute the ideal, to which all believers stand pledged; in him they become a band of 'brothers,' to whom Jesus is the one criterion of moral values[1]. With him lies the final award, and his coming will not tarry. To vindicate all wrongs, to recompense all endeavour, to award '*the crown of life*,' '*he stands the judge before the doors*' (i. 12 and v. 7–9—with which cf. Mt. xxiv. 33).

Thus, then, assuming objective sincerity and aim, and attaching due weight to omissions as well as to inclusions, a survey of the ethic yields much more positive result than at first seemed likely. As an address to Christians at Rome, or again to the Hellenic communities in Greece proper or Asia Minor, the Epistle would have little point or relevance; it would turn aside from outstanding evils to mere beating of the air. The ethic, as well as the language and surrounding, points clearly to Judaic outlook and Judaic background, it is the cry of nascent Christianity for emancipation, through a pure and reformed Judaism, from the intolerance, the class-feeling, and the religious prepossessions of a harsh and stereotyped hierarchy. To become intelligible, vital and coherent, not confused and shambling word-play, but a living whole instinct with spiritual strain, the Epistle must be associated with the surroundings of the Palestinian and Syrian synagogue, and the reactions that emanated from Jerusalem as the metropolis of Christian faith. So viewed, the emphasis on poverty gains specific point. The incipient community of possessions, narrated in A. ii. 44–5, iv. 34–7, the relief-fund raised at Antioch (A. xi. 22, 29–30), the systematic collections organised throughout the churches of Asia, Macedonia and Achaia, show the chronic straits of destitution to which the Christians at Jerusalem were subject: there it was that the relief of widows was a recognised

---

[1] Such is the significance of the striking and untranslateable τὸ καλὸν ὄνομα τὸ ἐπικληθὲν ἐφ᾽ ὑμᾶς (ii. 7), which—like ὁ ποιμὴν ὁ καλός—combines associations typically Greek and typically Hebraic. Again ἀδελφοί μου ἀγαπητοί (repeated i. 16, 19, ii. 5) is a *Christian* extension of the Jewish address ἀδελφοί, which occurs in every chapter.

part of the daily ministration[1]. What other church is likely to
have produced the antithetical aphorism '*Observance pure and
undefiled before God and the Father is this—to visit orphans and
widows in their affliction*' (i. 27)[2]? And the smarting reference to
labour conditions, agricultural oppression and the exactions of
owners (v. 4) is in natural accord with the realisation of farms,
small holdings and tenements recounted in A. iv. 34–7, v. 1,
and with the familiar background of Galilæan life. Things do
not fit so well by accident.

Note on James iii. 6

I wish that I could throw light on Jas. iii. 6 φλογίζουσα τὸν τροχὸν
τῆς γενέσεως καὶ φλογιζομένη ὑπὸ τῆς γεέννης—the standing crux of
commentators. The latter half of the clause fixes the meaning of
φλογίζειν. Associated with γεέννης it must mean to set on fire or
burn up, not to illuminate or irradiate; and this meaning has the
support of the LXX. It seems probable that the actual figure of
burning in the valley of Hinnom was present to the mind of the
writer. Gehenna occurs once only in the LXX, and then with a
purely topographical reference (Josh. xviii. 16). It becomes part
of the figurative language of apocalyptic and Rabbinic writers, but
was naturalised into Christian literature through the words of
Jesus, to which its use in N.T. is restricted. Its association here
with the tongue seems strange and unnatural.

The first half is more baffling still. In spite of one freakish
coincidence from an eighth-century writer[3], it seems impossible to
believe that the reference is to the ignition of chariot wheels by
friction with the axle: there is nothing in the context to suggest,
or to excuse it. Partial parallels extracted from Orphic or neo-
Platonic or Pythagorean language, referring to the wheel or cycle
of existence, are equally unconvincing[4]; cycles of metempsychosis
are entirely foreign to the context, and to any literary affinities
disclosed in the Epistle; and are quite out of keeping with 'the
tongue.' Nor does Hort's suggestion of connexion with the wheels

---

[1] A. vi. 1 ὅτι παρεθεωροῦντο ἐν τῇ διακονίᾳ τῇ καθημερινῇ αἱ χῆραι.

[2] The mere wording falls back on Scriptural precedent, e.g. ποιῶν κρίσιν
προσηλύτῳ καὶ ὀρφανῷ καὶ χήρᾳ (Deut. x. 18 and xxvii. 19), τοῦ πατρὸς
τῶν ὀρφανῶν καὶ κριτοῦ τῶν χηρῶν Ps. lxviii. 5, and Is. i. 17, etc., but
the inspiration of the precept comes from the surroundings.

[3] Achmet *Oneirocritica* 160.

[4] These are well summarised in Ropes *Internat. Crit. Comm.* pp. 237–9.

in the vision of Ezekiel open any door of interpretation. I have
searched in vain for any clues from medical or mystical or meta-
physical diction (Aristotelian, Platonic or neo-Platonic), and have
little doubt that the phrase takes its departure from the preceding
ἡλίκον πῦρ ἡλίκην ὕλην ἀνάπτει, not from some remote and un-
identified reference (unless it be Aramaic or Rabbinic). τροχός in
itself is susceptible of a great variety of meanings. Almost any
that is covered by English 'round' or 'run'—e.g. the round of
life or fate, the run of sap, or of timber—but none has yet been
found to give a convincing clue for this passage. And it would be
hard to improve on A.V. 'course of nature,' whatever that may mean.
More or less as a counsel of despair, I suggest that ὀπόν for τροχόν
would carry out the opening metaphor and give coherence to the
whole. The word is not Biblical, but is used metaphorically of
the sap and vigour, the vital forces, e.g. of youth (ἥβης); the meaning
would then be that the tongue, like a fire igniting a mass of wood,
sets on fire and burns up all the vital juices that contribute to the
making of man, and along the charred embers play the flickering
flames of Gehenna. This preserves for γένεσις that sense of man's
natural and spiritual growth, which it has in i. 23 and which we
should expect from the γεγονότας, 'made in the likeness of God,' in
v. 9; and does give intelligible and coherent expression to the sense
imputed to ὁ τροχός 'the wheel' as 'the impelling power of human
nature and life'; though apart from the unusualness of the word,
I can only adduce fanciful reasons for the replacement of ὀπόν by
τροχόν. If the unfamiliar ὀπόν were misread as ὄχον, it would
easily pass to τροχόν.

CHAPTER VI

DOCTRINE

We may now examine more minutely the sources from which James drew his convictions, and the use to which he puts them. There is no formulation of first principles, and the Epistle nowhere assumes the guise of a theological treatise, for which he had no training or equipment; but the opening section is so far systematic that it reveals the background of Jewish presuppositions from which the writer makes his ethical appeal. Throughout, as Hort was the first clearly to discern, it is based on the teaching of Genesis, and of that school of Pharisaic thought to which James was inured. Confusion has resulted from wresting his language into Pauline or Johannine moulds of thought, with which he was not familiar; and our English Version has suffered from the same mistaken bias.

The best popular account of contemporary Pharisaism is to be found in Josephus[1]. His father was of priestly lineage, highly esteemed in Jerusalem, and from boyhood Josephus had free intercourse with the inner circles of the official hierarchy[2]. His disposition was eclectic and inquisitive; at sixteen he attached himself to the Essene community, among whom for eight years he shared the rigours of the ascetic life. At nineteen (A.D. 56) an opening in civil administration brought him back to Jerusalem, where he finally threw in his lot with Pharisaism, which in moral aim he regards as a Jewish counterpart of Stoicism. More than once he defines in broad terms the distinguishing tenets of the three sects, all of which he knew from within, by experience

---

[1] Lightley *Jewish Sects and Parties in the Time of Christ* gives a full digest of the conflicting views and speculations of recent writers about the philosophic tenets of Pharisees, Sadducees, Essenes and others, together with their estimates of Josephus. There seems little reason to question the general trustworthiness of Josephus; and apart from his statements little solid standing-ground remains.

[2] Jos. *Vita* 1–2.

as well as observation. With their conflicting views upon Immortality, and upon the interpretation and authority of the Law,
we are not for the moment concerned. The third differentia
turned upon the problems of Moral Theism, and the relation
of the human nature to the Divine. The Essenes were ascetic
fatalists, who ascribed all that befalls—including all movements of
the Will—to overruling Fate or Destiny[1], the action of the Divine
providence. They lived in common under strict rules of diet,
dress and habit[2], and regarded death as the release of the soul from
its prison-house. The Sadducees[3], at the opposite pole, rejected
all belief in Immortality, and held that man's own Free-will was
the sole arbiter of his fate, and of his choice of good or evil.
The Pharisees took an intermediate position, which commanded
a far larger following[4]. "They maintained that all things were
the act of destiny: but none the less a wishing power belongs to
man, which contributes to the resultant impulse. It was God's
good pleasure that in concert with the ordinance of destiny the
will of man should act concurrently with virtue or with vice."[5]
Through the operation of this desire God used man's will for
carrying into effect his appointed ends. Logically the view presents
a compromise, the inner contradictions of which were not as yet
disclosed, and leave no trace upon the argument of our Epistle.
It opens, naturally enough, with reflexions on the nature and
origin of sin, and the meaning of temptation in the providential
ordering of life. 'My son, if thou settest forth to serve the Lord,
prepare thy soul for temptation'[6] is the exordium of the son of
Sirach, and must have been in the writer's mind, when he too
began '*Count it all joy, my brethren, when temptations manifold
beset you*' (i. 2). His object is to bring home to his readers the

---

[1] εἱμαρμένη *Ant.* XVIII. i. 5.   [2] *B. J.* II. viii. 2–11.

[3] *Ant.* XVIII. i. 4.   [4] *Ant.* XIII. x. 6.

[5] Jos. *B. J.* II. viii. 14, *Ant.* XIII. v. 9, XVIII. i. 3–6, are the leading
passages. In the latter it is worth noticing how little Josephus
adheres to the technical phraseology of contemporary Greek schools:
it has passed through a Jewish medium. πρασσέσθαι εἱμαρμένῃ τὰ πάντα
ἀξιοῦντες, οὐδὲ τοῦ ἀνθρωπείου τὸ βουλόμενον τῆς ἐπ' αὐτοῖς ὁρμῆς
ἀφαιροῦνται. δοκῆσαν τῷ θεῷ κρᾶσιν γενέσθαι καὶ τῷ ἐκείνης βουλευτηρίῳ
καὶ τῶν ἀνθρώπων τῷ θελήσαντι προσχωρεῖν μετὰ ἀρετῆς ἢ κακίας.

[6] Ecclus. ii. 1.

place of temptation in the divine scheme. Temptations have their use, and their abuse: their use, as designed by God for the discipline and perfecting of character (i. 3–4); their abuse, when man makes them the occasion for gratifying his own lower desires. And here, where James passes into the categories of Jewish theology, it will be well to give an exact rendering of the words he uses.

Let no man when tempted say 'It is of God that I am tempted' —for God is untempted of things evil, and himself tempteth no man; each man is tempted when drawn away by his own individual desire and enticed. Therewith the desire conceives and brings forth sin, and the sin when matured is big with death. Make no mistake, my brethren beloved. All [God's] giving is good, and every gift is perfect from above, coming down from the Father of lights, with whom is no variation nor shadowing of change. By act of will he did engender us by a word of truth, that we should be a kind of firstfruits of his creatures (i. 13–18).

This is none other than the current creed of Pharisaism, which, building on the Genesis record, attributed sin to the presence of the evil impulse (*yetzer hara*) or desire. This conception of sin as the prevalence of an innate propensity in the heart of man, is rooted in Rabbinic theology[1]. 'The imagination of man's heart is evil from his youth' (Gen. vi. 5, viii. 21). A few illustrations may be given from more or less contemporary writers. In the Fourth Book of Esdras, which belongs in substance to the first century, and owes something to Judaistic Christianity, we read: 'The first Adam, clothing himself with the evil heart (*cor malignum*—cf. Jer. xvii. 9), transgressed and was overcome; and likewise also all who were born of him...; the Law indeed was in the heart of the people, but side by side with it the evil germ; so what was good departed, and the evil remained' (4 Esdr. iii. 21–2, cf. vii. 116–18). Hence ensues the inveterate and wholesale tragedy of sin. But this propensity to sin is never actuated by God; it is the antithesis of His nature and being; '*God is untempted of things evil*'; they lie outside the Divine experience, and '*he*

[1] It is expounded at length in current authorities, e.g. Charles *Pseudepigrapha* ii. p. 555; Montefiore *Beginnings of Christianity* p. 54, *The Old Testament and After* pp. 118–25, 341.

himself tempteth no man.'[1] Temptation in every case means '*being drawn away and enticed by his own individual desire*'[2] (i. 15). And this desire or lust has the power of conceiving and bringing forth sin. Thereby 'Each one of us' in the language of the Book of Baruch[3], 'has become the Adam of his own soul.' The fault is not with God: '*All divine giving, and every particular gift is perfect from its heavenly source, as it comes down from the Father of lights.*'[4] Here, and later, the language is explicitly drawn from Genesis, the source to which Rabbinic learning turned for its rationale of sin, and in the following verse every word has reference to the original[5]. The 'act of will' referred to in βουληθείς is the divine resolve, 'Let us make man in our image, after our likeness' (Gen. i. 26), the charter of man's being, as he issued from the womb of creation. To refer the anarthrous λόγῳ ἀληθείας— '*a word of truth*'—to the message of the Gospel, or to the profession of belief, or to the elective call of God, makes havoc of the sense and of the Greek, while ἀπεκύησεν, 'was big with, was pregnant,' is one of the last terms one would expect of 'spiritual regeneration.' Rightly understood of the embryo man entering upon creature existence, the word and tense fall into their natural place, echoing not unsuitably the ἀποκνεῖ of i. 15. And the reference is clinched in the fine description of mankind as '*a kind of firstfruits of his creatures*' (i. 18), in which 'first-fruits' (ἀπαρχή) bears its specific thought of that part of the produce which is set apart for consecration, and the language recalls the phrasing of Wisdom—'Thou by thy wisdom didst fashion man to have

---

[1] i. 13 ὁ θεὸς ἀπείραστός ἐστιν κακῶν, πειράζει δὲ αὐτὸς οὐδένα. For the equivocal use of πειράζειν see p. 37.

[2] i. 14 ἕκαστος πειράζεται ὑπὸ τῆς ἰδίας ἐπιθυμίας ἐξελκόμενος καὶ δελεαζόμενος.

[3] 2 Baruch liv. 19. The *Apocalypse of Baruch*, an Apologia of Jewish Pharisaism, bears date A.D. 50–80 (see Charles *Pseudepigrapha* p. 512, and Introd. to 4 Ezra p. 554–6), and is therefore closely contemporary with the Epistle.

[4] i. 17. E.V. mistakes the predication and the sense. The reference to 'lights' is from Gen. i. 3, 14, 18, where φωστῆρες in LXX describes the celestial luminaries; but φῶτα is familiar from the Pss., and φῶς is used Gen. i. 3 (twice) and 18.

[5] i. 18 βουληθεὶς ἀπεκύησεν ἡμᾶς λόγῳ ἀληθείας, εἰς τὸ εἶναι ἡμᾶς ἀπαρχήν τινα τῶν αὐτοῦ κτισμάτων.

DOCTRINE 65

lordship over the creatures made by thee.'[1] If corroboration is
needed, it is to be found in the later verse, so fatally misconstrued
in E.V., where the irresponsive hearer of the word '*is like unto
a man, who regardeth the face of his genesis in a glass, and after so
regarding his proper self, goeth his way and straightway forgetteth
what manner of being he was.*'[2] '*The face of his genesis*' is a clear
and unmistakeable reference to the book of the Genesis of men: the
'glass,' which shows the lineaments of man's true being, is the
mirror of Scripture, the book of his 'Genesis' which reveals him
'as in a glass' to himself. St Paul's employment of the metaphor
(1 Cor. xiii. 12, and 2 Cor. iii. 18) supplies helpful illustrations,
but the figure is familiar to Rabbinic teaching[3] and probably
derived from thence. 'His *natural* (*sc.* bodily) face' is a despairing
and impossible perversion of the Greek and leaves the similitude
without intelligible sense, while '*the face of his genesis or origin*'—
which lends itself to copious illustration and comparisons—is an
interesting example of the stages by which τὸ πρόσωπον gradually
adapted itself to the later offices[4] in psychology and Christian
theology, which it was destined to discharge. In a rudimentary
form τὸ πρόσωπον τῆς γενέσεως is not far removed from 'the idea
of his personality' at a more developed stage of thought, but in
the simpler terms of St James is equivalent to '*the manner of
man that he was*' (ὁποῖος ἦν) as made in the image of God, where
ἦν (not ἐστί) must be credited with its proper value, '*was*' according to the design of God in his creation.

In all this there is no attempt at constructive theology, such as
meets us in the pages of St Paul or St John, or from a very different angle in the Epistle to the Hebrews. Neither from the side
of inner experience, nor from interpretations of the person of Jesus
Christ, does the writer propound new or transformed ideas of
redemption, or suggest any changed relationship to God resulting

---

[1] ἵνα δεσπόζῃ τῶν ὑπὸ σοῦ γενομένων κτισμάτων Wisd. ix. 2.
[2] Jas. i. 23 κατανοοῦντι τὸ πρόσωπον τῆς γενέσεως αὐτοῦ ἐν ἐσόπτρῳ.
In Gen. v. 1 the title name appears as ἡ βίβλος γενέσεως ἀνθρώπων.
[3] Wetstein on 1 Cor. xiii. 12.
[4] The same process may be traced in St Paul's use of ἐν προσώπῳ
Χριστοῦ (2 Cor. ii. 10, iv. 6); but the phrase must not tempt us into
prolonged digression.

R   5

66 DOCTRINE

from the manifestation, the Passion, Death or Resurrection of
Jesus. In Christology, even of an incipient kind, he falls far short
of the First Epistle of St Peter. But this must be reserved for
later consideration[1]. Here at least he abides within the fixed
framework of Jewish thought, and throughout with scrupulous
reference to words of Holy Writ. His treatment of sin is *ethical*
throughout: in common with all writers of the O.T., he abstains from
any reference to 'the Fall,' still more from speculative deductions
regarding its effect, such as make their appearance in the apocryphal writings[2], or from analogical inferences such as Paul (by
way of illustration rather than dogma) drew between the functions
of the first and of the second Adam. Still more remote from his
outlook are categories of original and wilful sin, of predestined
guilt, of prevenient or effectual grace, such as Augustine fathered
upon St Paul, and bequeathed with such unfortunate results to
Western and above all to Reformation theology.

Where then, it may pertinently be asked, can the impact of
Christianity[3] be traced in this Jewish manifesto? The answer is
not difficult. First and foremost, in precisely that direction which
the fabric of the Epistle would lead us to expect, in a revised and
authoritative ethic, derived from the teaching of Jesus, and expressed in a revaluation of Jewish Law. In matters of Jewish
practice and worship his reticence is no less marked than in those
of Christian. It is right and natural it should be so. For one
thing, these issues were of secondary importance; for another,
they inevitably provoked bitter disputes and recriminations; and
above all, it was not for him to intervene in decisions, which
belonged of right to other hands. His own injunctions are restricted to activities within the congregation, 'the synagogue' (ii
2, v. 13–16), which enjoyed almost unfettered latitude in teaching
and interior organisation. In his concentration upon the ethical,
he shuns all contentious and specific issues: there is no reference
to institutional or ceremonial Judaism, or to cardinal obligations

[1] Chap. VIII.
[2] In various forms, more or less explicit, as in 2 and 4 Esdr., Wisd.,
Ecclus., Baruch, Enoch, etc.
[3] With the help of two or three arbitrary excisions Spitta makes bold
to deny it altogether.

of circumcision, the Sabbath, and the whole regimen of ritual
observance. This must not be explained away as showing that
the Epistle was addressed to believers outside the range of the
Temple and the hierarchy: it is fundamental, inherent in the
writer's aim and mentality. His own headquarters were at the
very heart of observance and of conflict; but he neither impugns
nor enforces; his hopes were founded not upon institutional
enforcements, or surrenders, or compromises, but upon an ethical
advance and unification, which would remove the necessity for
such. The Law of Moses was destined to be absorbed in a higher
unity, in which it would be not abrogated but fulfilled. His
ancestral reverence for Law remains, but it is 'perfected' into
a higher law, which once again he speaks of as 'a law of liberty'
(i. 25, ii. 12), of Christian freedom realised in glad unquestioning
assent to the moral law involved in the sovereignty of God.
'*He that hath caught the vision of law perfected into the law of
liberty and abideth therein, becomes no more a hearer of forget-
fulness but a doer of the deed, and blessed shall he be in his doing
thereof*' (i. 25). The conception of freedom realised in the acceptance of Torah is familiar to O.T. and Rabbinic teaching, as
in 'I will walk at liberty; for I seek thy commandments' (Ps. cxix.
45) or again, 'I will run the way of thy commandments, when
thou hast set my heart at liberty' (Ps. cxix. 32); but it is hardly
open to question that in the Epistle this treatment of the Law
is directly derivative from the teaching of Jesus. The arresting
epithet (βασιλικός) '*kingly*' attached to Law (ii. 8) can hardly be
dissociated from the preaching of '*The Kingdom*' '*promised to them
that love him*' in the preceding verse (ii. 5). The attitude taken to
the Mosaic Law was in content and physiognomy one of the most
novel and distinctive features of the teaching of Jesus; yet almost
every instance and illustration of the same occurring in St James
finds a direct counterpart in the Sermon on the Mount. In one
passage, indeed, the detached injunction against oaths, '*Above all,
my brethren, swear not, neither by the heaven, nor by the earth,
nor by any other oath: but let your yea be yea, and your nay nay,
that ye fall not under judgment*' (v. 12), connexion with Mt. v.
33–7 seems at first sight unmistakeable. But the omissions and

the deviations are not less marked than the parallelism and prove
that the correspondence is due not to literary borrowing, but to
derivation from a common source. Both take their origin from
a current *Logion* of Jesus, which Matthew has recorded in fuller
and more authentic form: and the passage becomes an evidence
that the Epistle precedes the publication of the Gospel[1]. Parallels,
debts rather they may be termed, to the Sermon on the Mount
occur in great abundance[2]; but they are *not* of verbal expression,
but of moral content. They correspond to the stage of fluid oral
reminiscence, during which the *Logia* of Jesus were for a generation
preserved and handed down, until gradually through Q and other
sources they were combined by Matthew in the traditional form
exhibited in the Sermon on the Mount. This gives a natural
explanation of the close and numerous resemblances between the
Epistle and the Gospel, agreeing so closely in substance and
content, yet with a marked absence of verbal borrowing or
reproduction.

Confining Law to the range of moral commandments, inter-
preting them thus after the mind of Christ, and subjecting all
to the supremacy of the sovereign law '*Thou shalt love thy neighbour as thyself*' (ii. 8), it was still open to the Jewish Christian
to regard Torah as a progressive evolution in righteousness,
'whose end was Christ' (Rom. x. 4). His 'heart was set at liberty,'
and he could walk free from that yoke of literalism and legalism
which Christ had done away. It was a position which, within
these limits, St Paul's own polemic against the Law allowed and
indeed affirmed. In words that might have belonged, that in

---

[1] As it stands in our Epistle the passage is so jejune, so irrelevant, and
so interruptive of the general sense, that I cannot but regard it as an
intruding adscript or gloss, originally appended perhaps as comment
on iii. 9–10. This would in some measure account for the curtness of
form, and the unbalanced πρὸ πάντων: but it lacks manuscript support.
In Epistolary style πρὸ πάντων became a mere convention, calling
attention to some point, as in a postscript. For instances, see Robinson
on Ephesians p. 279. The alternative is to suppose it was a headline or note,
intended for further expansion; but what could be more unsatisfactory?
except, indeed, to connect it with the solemn protestations 'As God liveth,'
etc., to be found in the Book of Job! (See Maynard Smith p. 315.)

[2] Collected in Mayor's edition, pp. lxxxiv–v, and fully discussed in
Zahn I, pp. 89 f., 114, 121–2.

effect do belong, to the Epistle of St James, he too wrote (Rom. xiii. 8–10) 'He that loveth his neighbour hath fulfilled the law. For this Thou shalt not commit adultery, Thou shalt not kill, Thou shalt not steal, Thou shalt not covet, and if there be any other commandment, it is summed up in this word, namely Thou shalt love thy neighbour as thyself. Love worketh no ill to his neighbour; love therefore is the *fulfilment of the law*' (πλήρωμα νόμου). With that climax the Jewish Christian could remain content; the teaching of the Master was affirmed, not contravened; in a sense it was given exclusive possession: fidelity to Christ was no commission to provoke fresh issues, or to assail the treasured sanctions of tradition and authority, whose eventual destinies God alone, as in the past, could direct and overrule for 'the consolation of Israel.' '*Brethren, be not many teachers*' (iii. 1) is a pervading note of the Epistle, and nothing is more abhorrent to the writer than the temper of contentious and schismatic self-assertion. It was no more the calling of the Palestinian or Syrian Christian to assail the Jewish hierarchy and theocracy, than of the Roman Christian to declare war against the Imperial government or the rites of polytheism. St James' attitude to Law is characteristic and intelligible, and within his accepted limits consistent. Restricting his ministry to the children of Israel, and with regards fixed on ethical issues alone, he was able to leave ulterior questions in abeyance, and to rest within the lines laid down in the Sermon on the Mount. His attitude to 'Law' is that of the devout Jew, one of complete and unquestioning obedience—'*Whoso shall keep the whole law, yet stumble in one thing, is become guilty of all*'[1] (ii. 10); and even more expressly in iv. 11 '*If thou judgest the law, thou art not a doer of the law, but a judge. One only is the law-giver and the judge, even he who is able to save and to destroy.*' Under allegiance to the sovereign law (βασιλικὸς νόμος ii. 8), in obedience to the master-principle approved by Jesus Christ 'Thou shalt love thy neighbour as thyself,' the Christian enjoys that larger range of understanding and obedience, which James

[1] Mk. x. 21, Mt. xix. 21 carry the same suggestion, but the closest parallels are to be found in Rabbinic dicta, e.g. 'If a man do all, but omit one, he is guilty for all and each' by R. Jochanan.

twice over designates as '*law perfected—the law of liberty*.'[1] Beside
this paramount fidelity all lesser matters of the law sink into
insignificance.

The ethical revaluation of the Law leads on directly in Chap. ii
to the problem of belief and conduct, of Faith and Works. The
treatment of the theme is hardly more than parenthetical and
illustrative. The outlook remains directly ethical and practical.
But the form and conduct of the argument—'*But a man will
say...*,' '*But wilt thou know, O vain man...*'[2]—show plainly that
the relation of the two had already become matter of dispute.
James does not meet the problem by any psychological analysis
of 'faith,' but is content with simple affirmation of its ethical
values. Faith is an energy of will as well as heart, which by its
very nature must take effect in righteous action. In itself the
position is perfectly clear, but the side issues which it raises are
so far-reaching that they demand a chapter to themselves.

[1] i. 25 νόμον τέλειον τὸν τῆς ἐλευθερίας, ii. 12 διὰ νόμου ἐλευθερίας.
[2] ii. 18 ἀλλ' ἐρεῖ τις..., and ii. 20 θέλεις δὲ γνῶναι, ὦ ἄνθρωπε κενέ....
The form of question and answer here adopted are drawn from dialectical
debate.

CHAPTER VII

FAITH AND WORKS

'Faith' is a keyword in the transition from Hebraic to Christian theology. In its twofold combination of trust and belief, it has no exact counterpart in biblical Hebrew[1]: its nearest equivalent (Heb. *Amon*) occurs but rarely in the O.T., and does not rank among the saving or justifying attributes of soul-life. Nor is the reason far to seek. The ethical and spiritual ideals of Judaism were modelled upon the attributes of Jahweh, as gradually developed and conceived in the religious consciousness of Israel. But among these 'Faith'—as belief in his own existence, or as trust in his will for good, or as acceptance of his dispensations, or assurance of his power—could obviously have no place. Even in the capital proof text, 'The just shall live by faith' (Hab. ii. 4), the prophet did not mean that faith was the source or condition of righteousness, but that in face of all trials and reverses—the ruin, exile and extinction of the nation—the righteous would survive by faithfulness to the covenant of Jehovah, and to this primary sense Heb. x. 37–9 reverts in applying the text. The existence of Israel hung upon the maintenance of trust in Jehovah.

Essentially faith was the undefined but unquestioned basis on which religion rested, the presupposition of all Jahweh worship. There resided in the worshipper—'made in the image of God'— a spiritual capacity, or even a compelling intuition, able to discern the presence and handiwork of the Creator, to recognise his moral attributes, demands and purposes, and with them the will to comply with their requirements. Faith discerned a divine purpose in the created order of things, divine direction in the course of history, and a divine pledge in the covenant relation between Jahweh and the Israel of his choice. And the exercise of faith meant an inward assurance, an incontrovertible trust that God would on his side keep faith with his people, and that the promises

[1] Montefiore *O.T. and After* p. 171.

would find fulfilments. Thus in the Old Testament 'Faith' had
outgrown the merely fatalistic phase, which accepts and acquiesces
in the governance of God: it was an active power in life, a consciousness of God, a conviction registered within the Soul, the witness
and answer of man's spirit to the being and nature of God; it
was associated with deep ethical convictions; but it was not yet
recognised or named as an element in personality, and still less
were its implications argued or apprehended.

With the New Testament all is changed; 'Faith' gains new
status and position in the categories of religion; it becomes of
cardinal importance. The lines along which its content and implications are worked out are very different in St James, St Paul, the
Epistle to the Hebrews or St John; but in all alike 'faith' is a central
spring of spiritual forces and of co-operative union with God.
The conception of faith passes from that of static trust to that of
a dynamic inspiration. The change must be traced in part or in
whole to the direct teaching of Jesus, in which faith became a
central watchword, the secret and the source of saving power,
man's realisation of relationship with God, as in 'Thy faith hath
saved thee' (Mk. v. 34, x. 52, Mt. ix. 22, 29, L. vii. 50, viii. 48,
xvii. 19), 'Have faith in God' (Mk. xi. 22), 'Have ye not yet
faith?' (Mk. iv. 40), 'If ye have faith as a grain of mustard seed'
(L. xvii. 6, cf. Mt. xxi. 21), 'He could there do no mighty work,
because of their un-faith' (Mk. vi. 5–6 with Mt. xiii. 58). These
are but palmary texts[1] among many kindred utterances, by which
'faith' was naturalised into the religious vocabulary as best ex-
pressing man's personal relationship with the Divine. Just as
in the thought of sonship, 'obedience' was transmuted into love,
so too 'the fear of God' passed into the higher category of 'faith'
in God.

St James supplies the earliest and simplest presentment of this
teaching, as envisaged by Jewish Christians. Outside of ch. ii
the word occurs three times in the Epistle. In i. 3 it stands in
the very forefront, as the term which best denotes the believer's
relationship to God. The phrase employed, '*the proof of your*

[1] For others, cf. Mk. xvii. 17, ix. 19, Mt. xiv. 31, xv. 28, xvi. 8, xvii. 20,
ὀλιγόπιστος.

faith worketh endurance,'[1] is arresting and impressive; it means that when trust in God is put to the proof—the test of conduct —and holds, it produces, results in, the temper of persistency, tenacity, endurance. For those to whom James wrote, that was its spiritual value. The two other passages[2] may be bracketed together, insisting upon 'faith' as a condition of efficacious prayer. The first is direct reminiscence of words of Jesus—'Ask and it shall be given to you,' and 'If ye have faith and doubt not,'[3] used in the same connexion as that of our Epistle; while the second refers directly to the precedents of healing furnished by the Galilæan ministry.

In ch. ii James is drawn on to a discussion upon the relation between 'faith' and 'works'—belief and conduct. In a religion so ethical in demand and so insistent upon observance as that of Judaism, the question could not but arise. It is often stated that the antithesis between Faith and Works had become a stock theme for Rabbinical discussion[4]; but for this no sufficient evidence is forthcoming, though it is true to say that (in discussions on Gen. xv. 6 and elsewhere) Philo and the Alexandrines give more and more prominence to 'Faith'— that is, 'trust in God'—as a constituent part of godliness (εὐσέβεια). The discussion was native to the soil of early Christianity, a resultant from the teaching of Jesus; and one aspect of the contrast between the Law and the Gospel. But in his dealing with faith and works James moves within the circle of O.T. presuppositions, to which any thought of conflict or opposition between the two was foreign[5]. They were twins, going hand in hand. Faith is the recognition of the being and prerogatives of

[1] τὸ δοκίμιον ὑμῶν τῆς πίστεως κατεργάζεται ὑπομονήν.

[2] i. 6 αἰτείτω δὲ ἐν πίστει, μηδὲν διακρινόμενος. v. 15 ἡ εὐχὴ τῆς πίστεως σώσει τὸν κάμνοντα, καὶ ἐγερεῖ αὐτὸν ὁ Κύριος. Immediately preceded by ἐν τῷ ὀνόματι τοῦ Κυρίου—even if WH are correct in omitting τοῦ Κυρίου—ὁ Κύριος unmistakeably refers to Jesus. For ἐγερεῖ αὐτὸν ὁ Κύριος cf. προσελθὼν ἤγειρεν αὐτήν Mk. i. 31.

[3] αἰτεῖτε καὶ δοθήσεται ὑμῖν Mt. vii. 7, and ἐὰν ἔχητε πίστιν καὶ μὴ διακριθῆτε Mt. xxi. 21, cf. Mk. xi. 23 ὃς ἂν εἴπῃ...καὶ μὴ διακριθῇ ἐν τῇ καρδίᾳ ἀλλὰ πιστεύσῃ...ἔσται αὐτῷ ὃ ἐὰν εἴπῃ. Cf. p. 55 n.

[4] Compare Lightfoot *Galatians* p. 157, Mayor *Ep. James* pp. clix ff., Farrar *Early Days of Christianity* pp. 351, 353 with Hort *Ep. James* xxv, p. 166 n., Sanday and Headlam *Romans* pp. 102-5.

[5] Montefiore *O.T. and After* pp. 169, 173, 176.

God, and functions as trust obedient to the intimations of his will; it is the motive power which impels the will and supplies the resolution to fulfil the commands of God and to walk in his ways. At this early stage the Law consisted of the few and fundamental prescriptions, 'the commandments' which set forth the moral relations between man and God, and man and his fellow-men. It could justly be summarised in the twofold commandment of Love to God and Love to neighbour, to which Jesus reverted as fulfilling the substance of the Law. Not until the post-prophetic period, when the Law was expanded and elaborated, classified into groups and series of enactments, moral and ritual, did the danger of the process become apparent. The intention was to clarify the requirements it imposed, to provide guiding rules with authoritative sanctions and prohibitions, and so make it applicable to the daily round of duty: but the actual result was to supersede and gradually supplant the moral instincts, to cripple and paralyse the free play of conscience, and substitute for it the rules and the restrictions of specialists and casuists, to transform morality into legalism, formulated as a dry and soulless network of conventions and routines[1]. The Rabbis enumerated 248 classes of things to be done, 365 of things forbidden: each attempt at amendment and simplification seemed only to aggravate the evil, and to provide new material for the wrangling controversies of the disciples of Hillel and of Shammai. This was the phase of law which provoked the denunciations of Jesus, and against which the polemic of St Paul was at heart directed. James stands for the age of transition, reluctant to break away from the old moorings, and clinging to the belief that the breach did not go beyond verbal controversies, such as could be averted or closed by mutual charity. It was not for him to wake doctrinal issues in his effort to secure single-hearted application of Christian belief in the practice of Christian profession. They enter as a mere parenthesis, free of controversial intent.

At the outset, the emphasis is thrown upon '*not with respect of persons.*' His concern is to eliminate worldly motives and distinctions from the exercise of Christian society and worship. '*No

[1] Montefiore *O.T. and After* p. 230 f.

respect of persons'[1] is a condition essential to '*the faith of our Lord Jesus Christ'*: the two are incompatible, 'ye cannot serve God and Mammon.' About the true interpretation of the phrase '*to faith of our Lord Jesus Christ*' there can be no doubt. It is questionable whether it is ever used to express '*faith in Christ,*' as conveyed by the Pauline 'in Christ' (ἐν Χριστῷ), or the Johannine 'believe in' (πιστεύειν εἰς). In any case such use is rare, and distinctively Pauline[2]. But here, apart from any parallel in James, such rendering is alien to the context: faith in Christianity has no clear connexion with 'respect of persons': the 'faith' to which he appeals is the faith taught, inculcated, demanded and exemplified by Jesus Christ, a faith that rests on direct and recognised relationship with God, and which eschews competing claims of position, outward respect, or exterior privilege.

The connecting thread with what follows—though the logical texture is by no means close—consists in loyalty to God, displayed in ready and unquestioning acceptance and obedience to his will. This must be without reserve, '*Whosoever stumbleth in one point, is guilty of all*' (ii. 10), and must take effect in act. That is the crucial test. Belief that stops short at profession, or at sentiment, or at intellectual assent[3], is unprofitable; '*faith without works is of none effect.*' Until it passes into an operative exercise of will, and bears fruit in act, faith remains '*dead in itself*' (νεκρὰ καθ' ἑαυτήν (ii. 17)), a potentiality, not yet a living or a saving power (ii. 14). The conclusion is clinched by appeal to the precedents of Abraham and of Rahab. Each '*was accounted just as the result of works,*'[4] that is to say, realised righteousness in a

---

[1] ii. 1 μὴ ἐν προσωπολημψίαις ἔχετε τὴν πίστιν, reiterated in ii. 9.

[2] Rom. iii. 22, Gal. ii. 16, 20, iii. 2, Phil. iii. 9 are the most pertinent passages.

[3] For faith as lip-profession ii. 14 ἐὰν πίστιν λέγῃ τις ἔχειν; as sentiment ii. 16 ὑπάγετε ἐν εἰρήνῃ, θερμαίνεσθε καὶ χορτάζεσθε; as intellectual assent ii. 19 τὰ δαιμόνια πιστεύουσι, καὶ φρίσσουσι. In ii. 20 nearly all editors agree in reading ἡ πίστις χωρὶς τῶν ἔργων ἀργή ἐστι, and so the Revised Version. If we remember the etymology (from ἀεργος) the phrase is almost a tautology, but the word had long since contracted its lower implications of idle, worthless, good-for-nothing, unprofitable. Cf. the contemptuous γαστέρες ἀργαί quoted in Tit. i. 12.

[4] ii. 21, 25 ἐξ ἔργων ἐδικαιώθη and ii. 22 καὶ ἐκ τῶν ἔργων ἡ πίστις ἐτελειώθη.

course or piece of conduct. Action is the criterion of the presence
and reality of faith, and the perfecter of its being. Their examples
are a proof that '*faith without works is dead*' (*v.* 26). The final
paragraph (*v.* 17–26) it will be seen is not the culmination of an
argument, but a corroborative illustration used to enforce his
ethical appeal. It is a humble instance of that typically Hebraic
appeal to history, which adorns the Books of Psalms (esp. Ps.
lxxviii, cv, cvi), of Ecclesiasticus (xliv–xlix) and of Maccabees
(1 Macc. ii), and which attains yet more elaborate and copious
developments in Philo and in the Epistle to the Hebrews. Here,
the terms throughout retain their simplest signification[1]; the
whole approach and handling of the argument is practical and
ethical; there is no attempt at formulating theology or constructing
a scheme of salvation. No sort of specific merit or sanction is
attached to 'works,' for instance as 'Works of the Law'; nor does
'faith' involve prescribed forms of thought or creed or institutional observance: the two terms are not antithetical, but comple-
mentary, companion outputs, related as cause and effect—as germ
and fruit—'faith' the antecedent, 'works' the consequent; effect
is the one sure evidence of cause, and without cause effect is
impossible. '*Show me thy faith apart from thy works, and I by
my works will show thee my faith*' (ii. 18). There is no hint of
any polemic balancing one against the other, and ascribing higher
value to this or that component in an indivisible whole: for faith
to be accounted righteousness, it must fruit in works. The thought
remains throughout within the circle of O.T. ideas. Of the two
phrases that have a flavour of later controversy, one—'*imputed
unto him for righteousness*' (ii. 23) is explicitly quoted from
Gen. xv. 6[2], and it recurs in Ps. cvi. 30, and in 1 Macc. ii. 52
is put in the forefront of the dying charge of Mattathias, adjuring
his sons to keep faithful to the religion of their fathers. It is in

---

[1] Strikingly shown in the selection of Rahab, among all the heroes of
the faith, as an exemplary instance. In Heb. xi. 31, followed by 1 Clem.
Rom. xii. 1, 'Ραὰβ ἡ πόρνη is similarly singled out as an example of
faith.

[2] The simple ἐλογίσθη 'accounted' of Gen. xv. 6 has no suggestion of
the implications and associations which attach to the 'imputed' of
sixteenth-century controversies.

FAITH AND WORKS 77

fact, as recognised by James and Paul[1], the standard text associating righteousness with faithfulness, in the representative—and one may add, symbolic[2]—figure of 'faithful' Abraham, the father of the faithful.

The phrase '*justified by works*' (ii. 21) stands on another footing; it is not derived from Scripture, but is, so far as our evidence goes, of St James' own invention, his brief inference or summary from the record in Genesis. In the earlier and historic books the verb (δικαιοῦσθαι) occurs but seldom, but found increasing favour in the later books—in deutero-Isaiah, in the Psalms, in Ecclesiasticus—correlated with that noun and adjective, 'righteousness' and 'righteous' which gained so central a position in the ethics of Israel. Throughout the LXX the verb has always the same meaning, to be approved, declared, pronounced righteous, whether the verdict proceed from God (as Judge), or from the moral sense of the community, or from the award of history. 'Neither by formation,' nor by usage, does it signify 'to be made righteous.'[3] And to this usage James unmistakeably adheres—'*By works, conduct, his righteousness was approved, when he offered his son Isaac upon the altar*' (ii. 21); and even more explicitly in ii. 23-4, where '*It was accounted to him for righteousness*' is immediately paraphrased by '*Ye see that it is by works, conduct, that a man is approved righteous....*' The phrase once minted is so compact and forcible that it was sure to become current coin, and would lend itself to any meaning or development attained by the verb itself (δικαιοῦσθαι 'justify'). We see the process in St Paul, who, while deriving the word from the O.T., invests it with a new sense, and in two separate Epistles seems to attribute to the Psalmist '*By works of the law shall no flesh be justified,*' a pronouncement which rests on words inserted by himself[4].

[1] Cited in Rom. iv. 3, 5, 9, 22, and Gal. iii. 6.
[2] In Philo, on whose frequent use of the text, see Lightfoot *Galatians* pp. 157-8.
[3] Sanday and Headlam *Ep. Romans* pp. 28-31.
[4] In Ps. cxlii. 2 the LXX runs ὅτι οὐ δικαιωθήσεται ἐνώπιόν σου πᾶς ζῶν, while in Gal. ii. 16, and again Rom. iii. 20, Paul adduces it as a proof text for his doctrine of justification by faith, in the form ὅτι ἐξ ἔργων νόμου οὐ δικαιωθήσεται πᾶσα σὰρξ ἐνώπιον αὐτοῦ. No excuse has been found for this bold manipulation of the text.

At a certain stage, when religion seeks to co-ordinate its beliefs
with the teachings of psychology, the phrase 'justified by works'
becomes in a sense so apt and obvious, that it might easily have
occurred to different minds; but in practice, such phrases usually
originate with an individual, and are quickly caught up from a
sense of their fitness. That a literary connexion exists between
our Epistle and that to the Romans is demonstrable, and the
precedence, wherever tests are applicable, seems to rest with James.
The evidence does not rest on a single phrase such as this, but
is cumulative: proofs of literary relationship hinge so entirely
upon exact and scholarly appreciation of the original Greek, that
I relegate them to an Appendix[1]; but the result is of cardinal
importance for determining the true relation between the writers
and their ways of thought. If Paul in writing to the Romans was
acquainted with the Epistle of James, it follows that James is
not attempting to confute the terms or arguments of that Epistle:
he is relieved of charges little creditable to his intelligence or
spiritual insight. In dealing with faith and works, his aims, his
interest, his inspiration are wholly ethical: doctrinally, the whole
cast of his mind is conservative; he stands upon the ancient ways;
earnestly, devoutly steeped in 'the traditions of the fathers,'[2] and
deriving thence his terms and his ideals; on the ethical side he
remains loyal to Judaism, as interpreted and to some extent—
more indeed than he perceived—revised by the authoritative
genius of Jesus Christ. But the person of Jesus does not suggest
to him any need for theological reconstruction or advance. So
far as they retain ethical authority and value, the old forms and
words suffice; he has no inclination to alter or reinterpret the
term 'faith,' provided only that it functions ethically, that it
works, that it yields practical results. Throughout there is no
suggestion of broaching or confuting any new doctrine of 'faith,'
or of engaging in any conflict with Pauline speculation or dialectic.
New issues were forced upon Paul by his repudiation of Jewish
Law, and there is no reason to suppose that the corollaries of
Gentile and Hellenic thought would have had interest or meaning
for the general body of Jewish Christians. The direct and vital

---

[1] App. pp. 84–87.   [2] Gal. i. 14.

differences turned upon obligations, ordinances and ceremonies, about which James stedfastly keeps silence. From the first beginnings of his missionary career Paul and James had occasions of personal intercourse, and there were far more acute differences of practice and Church discipline, in which they agreed to differ, and in which Paul as Apostle to the Gentiles received countenance from James in going his own way. The problems, the influences, the forms of thought and of belief, which Paul was called upon to face, lay outside the range of James. In relation to Jewish Law, James' prime concern was consistency of Christian conduct and belief. There are commentators who impute to James a correction of antinomian tendencies consequent on the teaching of Paul. His own words contain no hint of any such intention, nor would he in such case have singled out Rahab as his supporting example of effectual faith. His note is not controversial, but positive and hortatory, a call to his readers to rise above a futile and inoperative faith to the levels which their belief demands and to the full courage of their convictions.

The precise attitude of Paul is more difficult to gauge or to divine. It is no mere question of controversial methods or manner: considerations of motive, of temperament, of mentality, of relations public and private between the leaders of separate churches and types of Christian thought, come in; the particular circumstances of composition and intention in the Epistles are important. Those who best realise the complexity and the incompleteness of the data will be the last to expect to see eye to eye at all points with other inquirers, or to claim finality for their own conclusions. Yet assuming the priority of James, the relation seems to me clear. From the ethical side Paul treats the Epistle of James with marked respect: like Peter, he pays the tribute of adaptation to his opening utterance; he incorporates more than one of the most telling and distinctive phrases; he shares and summarises his ethical foundations: if the anachronism may pass, Paul and Peter are the first attestors of his claim to canonicity. Within James' own limits, those of a refined monotheistic Judaism, there is complete and express accord: phrases such as 'a transgressor of law,' 'a righteousness of God' (Rom. i. 17, iii. 21, etc.), the emphasis laid upon presumptuous 'judging' and presumptuous 'teaching,' still more the thought of law as the sovereignty of the principle of love and the realisation of moral freedom[1], are resemblances of a striking kind; and on the broad issue Paul is no more confuting James than he is confuting the words of his own Epistle: 'There is no respect of persons with God: for not the hearers of law are just before God, *but the doers of law shall be justified*' (Rom. ii. 11, 13), words which any reader might be excused for ascribing to St James.

Only when Paul presses on to new regions of analysis foreign to James do contradictions begin to emerge[2]: and of them it may be said (1) that they rest upon altered content of the terms employed, and (2) that they are nowhere aimed at James in particular[3], but are inherent in that fundamental reinterpretation of Judaism by which Paul effected the transition to Christianity. He is not a systematic theologian, building up a coherent scheme from deductive reasonings or historical premisses, but the recipient of vital and decisive experiences and reactions, of which he tries to render, to himself and other men, the clearest account of which he is capable. In the light of those experiences, from the Conversion onwards, religion became to him Christocentric[4] through and through. In the incarnate, risen and glorified Jesus all previous revelations of God were superseded and eclipsed: every relation of man to God—in respect of sin, forgiveness, communion and service—was mediated through Him: all was 'in Christ' (ἐν Χριστῷ), the source and satisfaction of all spiritual

---

[1] With Jas. ii. 8 νόμον τελεῖτε βασιλικόν cf. Rom. ii. 27 κρινεῖ...τὸν νόμον τελοῦσα σέ...παραβάτην νόμου, and Rom. xiii. 8–9. It is noticeable how the closest parallels belong to the Epistle to the Romans. The προσωπολημψία of Rom. ii. 11 might be added, but occurs elsewhere. For more detailed discussion, see pp. 67 and 84–5. With ἐλευθερία of Jas. i. 25, ii. 12 compare Gal. v. 1, 2 Cor. iii. 17, Rom. viii. 2, etc.

[2] Cf. Stevens *Pauline Theol.* pp. 284–5: 'In his own writings the forensic aspect of justification needs to be harmonised with the ethical, by recognising differences of connotation in his use of the term.'

[3] *Per silentium* Paul seems at pains to avoid, not seek, any touch of personal polemic.

[4] Harnack *Hist. Dogma* i. 135 (*ap.* Wood *Life, Letters and Religion* p. 399). Rostron *Christology of St Paul* pp. vii, 208–9, 227.

energies. This is no place to expatiate upon the whole scheme, but simply to point out its bearing upon the problem of 'faith' and 'works.' In the process it was inevitable that he should reinterpret, and in no small degree recast the content of faith, for its place in his Christocentric synthesis.

Along the lines of Jewish thought 'faith' meant the trustful acceptance of God's will[1], with the assurance that it was for the best. 'Commit thy way unto the Lord, and put thy trust in him, and he shall bring it to pass.'[2] As such, in the nation and in the individual, it had scaled heroic heights of resolution and of sacrifice, but there was always the fear of it falling back upon the plane of the purely submissive virtues—humility, patience, resignation and the rest—and so relapsing into passive forms, or into lifeless lip-profession. That meant 'the *death*' of faith, which must function *in action*, to remain alive. This was the danger against which James warns his readers; faith must remain '*full of good fruits, without doubting and without pretence*,' if it was to bring forth '*fruit of righteousness*' (iii. 18). Paul does not discard or contradict the old categories; that works follow upon faith, as light from sunrise, Paul would be the last to deny[3]. But as an essential corollary of his Christocentric thought, he proceeds to a more searching exegesis and gives a new orientation and extension of functions to the term 'faith.' When Jehovah, God of the Jews, was interpreted anew in terms of Christ, faith found a new and corresponding centre of gravity. It was transformed from instinctive and unquestioning trust into a conscious personal relation, embodied and accessible in Jesus Christ. From Him faith draws its living springs of energy, as a vital reaction of affection, will and act to the momentum initiated by Christ. It realises that *inwardness* of motive[4], which according to Jesus was

---

[1] It is a mistake to define it as 'theoretical belief'; it is practical and operative *conviction*—faith operating, made operative through love—πίστις δι' ἀγάπης ἐνεργουμένη Gal. v. 6.

[2] Ps. xxxvii. 5.

[3] The insistence on 'good works' is repeated in every group of his Epistles—so in 2 Thes. ii. 17; in 2 Cor. ix. 8 and Rom. ii. 6, 7, xii–xiii; in Eph. ii. 10 and Col. i. 10; in 1 Tim. vi. 18 and Tit. ii. 7, 14, iii. 8.

[4] Scott *Ethical Teaching of Jesus* p. 19.

the index of all moral quality. Faith is the sensitive response to a new centre of attractive and compelling energy, the appropriation of its forces, functioning in every exercise of desire, volition and behaviour. It is the operative antecedent of every Christian act: it cannot drop into mere static, or inert, acceptance; for its very being is responsive and dynamic: 'dead faith' becomes a contradiction jn terms: it is like talking of 'dead life.'

Further, in this Christocentric polemic, Paul introduces a still more definite restriction into his use of the term 'Works.' Elsewhere, just as in James, the term is used again and again in its ordinary acceptation of action and behaviour; few words are commoner in Pauline vocabulary; but in the passages under consideration in the Epistles to the Galatians and the Romans, 'Works' either explicitly (as in Gal. ii. 16, iii. 2, 5, 10—Rom. iii. 27–8) or by the context (Rom. iv. 2–6) connote definitely '*Works of the Law*,' consisting in prescribed obediences to an external regimen of enforcements and prohibitions, to which saving virtue was attached. The Pauline doctrine of justification by Faith arises directly out of his contention for Gentile liberation from the Law. Conduct is subjected to a new sanction; compliance with the mind of Jesus, attained solely through '*faith*,' takes the place of compliance with the requirements of the Law. It was a daring innovation on the traditional outlook, and in dispossessing the sacred Torah, it appeared to deny the spiritual prerogatives and monopolies of Israel; it is no wonder that it provoked implacable resentment and recrimination, for it raised the issue: Should Christianity remain a department of Judaism, or in its own right claim the world?

Of these deeper problems our Epistle shows no trace. On the ethical side, James rested in a tentative solution, which accepted as authoritative the spiritual restatements of Mosaic Law, propounded by Jesus. On the more fundamental issues raised by circumcision, by the ceremonial rules touching clean and unclean, and by the whole sacrificial system, he forbears to touch; and the silence must be deliberate: for Jewish Christians, for proselytes, and for worship of the synagogue, they did not immediately arise, and Jerusalem was the last place where a peaceable solution could be expected; reconciliation spelt unconditional surrender. Throughout his handling of the theme seems to exclude the idea of considered conflict with St Paul: he ignores his dialectic, and shows no understanding of its content or terms. They lie outside his own horizon. It would have been easy to raise objections, or to marshal texts, adverse to a thesis so novel and so revolutionary. On the contrary, in dealing with the example of Abraham, James founds himself upon the very text 'Abraham believed, and it was counted to him for righteousness,' which Paul most stressed in favour of his own restatement. In his second illustration, drawn from Rahab, he selects the very instance most susceptible of antinomian applications. As illustrations of his own thesis, the need of *operative* faith, they serve their end; they are picturesque and telling; they reappear in the splendidly elaborated appeal of the Epistle to the Hebrews: but as a reasoned refutation of Paul's argument, they are negligible: they involve complete want of comprehension in the writer. This argument has indeed been pressed, not without cogency, by those who advocate a late date, as a reason for relegating the Epistle to a period later than Clement or even Hermas. The 'blanched Christology'[1] and the incapacity to grasp the Pauline scheme of redemption belong, it is said, to the period of the *Didache* or the letter to Diognetus, when the inspirations of Apostolic Christianity were fading into the invertebrate and enfeebled moralisings of the sub-Apostolic age. The hypothesis is beset by fatal objections[2], and the simple fact of priority gives a far better clue to the failure of appreciation. The doctrinal shortcomings of the Epistle are primitive, not archaistic. It is indeed 'the most un-Pauline book in the New Testament,' but because it is pre-Pauline, not because it has forgotten and outlived the Pauline inspiration.

[1] Moffatt *Introd. N.T.* p. 471.
[2] On these see Chap. XI.

ON THE LITERARY RELATIONS OF THE EPISTLE OF JAMES AND THE EPISTLE TO THE ROMANS

A synopsis of verbal parallels between the two Epistles is supplied by Mayor[1]. In examining the links of literary connexion, we may found ourselves upon the salient instances. Fainter reflexions or correspondences will then assume their proper values.

(1) In structural form, and in the elements of language used, it seems hardly possible to dissociate εἰδότες ὅτι ἡ θλίψις ὑπομονὴν κατεργάζεται ἡ δὲ ὑπομονὴ δοκιμήν, ἡ δὲ δοκιμὴ ἐλπίδα κ.τ.λ. (Rom. v. 4) from the less finished γιγνώσκοντες ὅτι τὸ δοκίμιον ὑμῶν τῆς πίστεως κατεργάζεται ὑπομονήν, ἡ δὲ ὑπομονὴ ἔργον τέλειον ἐχέτω... of Jas. i. 3–4. The higher finish, and the closer analysis of ethical experience, is what we might expect from Paul, but this could hardly revert into the cruder original of James; the cut diamond does not relapse into the raw jewel: and a verbal detail has convincing significance. τὸ δοκίμιον is the LXX term (Ps. xi. 6, Prov. xxvii. 21) utilised by James; Paul amends it to his own more classical δοκιμή, which has no place in LXX; while 1 Pet. i. 7 adheres to the James original. Under the prompting of Paul, James could hardly have substituted τὸ δοκίμιον for the neater and more antithetical δοκιμή, and a small point like this goes far to determine priority.

(2) Jas. i. 22 γίνεσθε ποιηταὶ λόγου καὶ μὴ ἀκροαταὶ μόνον receives from James an aphoristic form, for which the LXX supplies no precedent, and the words themselves occur but seldom. James plays round the epigram in i. 25 οὐκ ἀκροατής...γενόμενος ἀλλὰ ποιητὴς ἔργου, and again in iv. 11 οὐκ εἰ ποιητὴς νόμου. Paul uses it once only[2], as though ready to his hand in finished form οὐ γὰρ οἱ ἀκροαταὶ νόμου δίκαιοι παρὰ τῷ θεῷ ἀλλ' οἱ ποιηταὶ νόμου δικαιωθήσονται (Rom. ii. 13). In the last clause the emphatic praise of 'law-doers,' and the non-technical use of δικαιοῦσθαι are a summary endorsement of James' own contention in ii. 14 ff. In the immediate neighbourhood (Rom. ii. 11) we find οὐ γάρ ἐστι προσωπολημψία παρὰ τῷ θεῷ in close verbal agreement with Jas. ii. 1 μὴ ἐν προσωπολημψίαις ἔχετε τὴν πίστιν (though its

---

[1] Mayor pp. xcv–xcvi.

[2] There is no other use of ἀκροαταί in N.T.

recurrence in Eph. vi. 9, Col. iii. 25 suggests some proverbial background): while a few verses later παραβάτης νόμου (ii. 25, 27) is a close and striking repetition of Jas. ii. 11 γέγονας παραβάτης νόμου (cf. ii. 9), which occurs nowhere else in LXX or N.T. Indeed, this section of the Epistle, Rom. ii. 1–16, contains constant reminders—conscious or unconscious—of the words and manner of St James. For instance: ii. 1 ὦ ἄνθρωπε πᾶς ὁ κρίνων· ἐν ᾧ γὰρ κρίνεις τὸν ἕτερον, σεαυτὸν κατακρίνεις and ὦ ἄνθρωπε ὁ κρίνων (ii. 3) compared with the ὦ ἄνθρωπε κενέ of Jas. ii. 20, and Jas. iv. 11 ὁ κρίνων τὸν ἀδελφὸν...κρίνει νόμον· εἰ δὲ νόμον κρίνεις, οὐκ εἶ ποιητὴς νόμου, ἀλλὰ κριτής... σὺ δὲ τίς εἶ ὁ κρίνων τὸν πλησίον; which is reproduced *verbatim* σὺ τίς εἶ ὁ κρίνων in Rom. xiv. 4. While διὰ νόμου κριθήσονται of Rom. ii. 12 is still further paralleled by ὡς διὰ νόμου ἐλευθερίας μέλλοντες κρίνεσθαι of Jas. ii. 12.

(3) Rom. ii. 5 θησαυρίζεις σεαυτῷ ὀργὴν ἐν ἡμέρᾳ σφαγῆς reads like an echo from James. Only here, and in the πῦρ ἐθησαυρίσατε ἐν ἐσχάταις ἡμέραις of Jas. v. 3 is θησαυρίζειν used in N.T. of storing up that which is evil and destructive. It has the sanction of O.T. usage, as in οἱ φόνου μετέχοντες θησαυρίζουσιν ἑαυτοῖς κακά Prov. i. 18, and so far as the single word is concerned, the correspondence between Paul and James might be accidental; but when we find ἐν ἡμέρᾳ σφαγῆς following only two verses later (in Jas. v. 5), the evidence of conscious or unconscious reminiscence becomes irresistible. Posteriority rests plainly with Paul, who combines the detached expressions into a single phrase.

In Greek, as in our English version, the words of James have an arresting quality, a bite that fastens them easily in the memory. ἀνυπόκριτος for instance, though it does occur in Wisdom, passes into Pauline (Rom. xii. 9, 2 Cor. vi. 6) and Petrine (1 P. i. 22) vocabulary through James (iii. 17), and is thus derivable from the teaching of Jesus. James was one at least of the media through which Paul gained his knowledge of the fundamental teaching of Jesus in relation to traditional Judaism, and of his personality as displayed in meekness, gentleness and humility[1].

(4) As containing the gist of Christian ethic, Rom. xiii. 8–10

---

[1] With πραΰτης (Jas. iii. 13) compare 1 Cor. iv. 21, 2 Cor. x. 1, Gal. vi. 1, Eph. iv. 2; with ἐπιεικής (Jas. iii. 17) compare 2 Cor. x. 1, Phil. iv. 5; with ταπεινοῦν and correlatives (Jas. i. 9, 10, iv. 6, 10) compare Phil. ii. 3, ii. 8, Col. iii. 2 and kindred passages.

may fairly be described as a Pauline résumé of Jas. ii. 8–11, and careful comparison points unmistakeably to literary obligation:

ὁ γὰρ ἀγαπῶν τὸν ἕτερον νόμον πεπλήρωκεν. τὸ γὰρ Οὐ μοιχεύσεις, Οὐ φονεύσεις, Οὐ κλέψεις, Οὐκ ἐπιθυμήσεις, καὶ εἴ τις ἑτέρα ἐντολή, ἐν τῷ λόγῳ τούτῳ ἀνακεφαλαιοῦται, ἐν τῷ Ἀγαπήσεις τὸν πλησίον σου ὡς ἑαυτόν. ἡ ἀγάπη τῷ πλησίον κακὸν οὐκ ἐργάζεται· πλήρωμα οὖν νόμου ἡ ἀγάπη. Rom. xiii. 8–10.

εἰ μέντοι νόμον τελεῖτε βασιλικὸν κατὰ τὴν γραφήν Ἀγαπήσεις τὸν πλησίον σου ὡς σεαυτόν, καλῶς ποιεῖτε· εἰ δὲ προσωπολημπτεῖτε, ἁμαρτίαν ἐργάζεσθε, ἐλεγχόμενοι ὑπὸ τοῦ νόμου ὡς παραβάται. ὅστις γὰρ ὅλον τὸν νόμον τηρήσῃ, πταίσῃ δὲ ἐν ἑνί, γέγονε πάντων ἔνοχος. ὁ γὰρ εἰπών Μὴ μοιχεύσῃς εἶπεν καί Μὴ φονεύσῃς· εἰ δὲ οὐ μοιχεύεις φονεύεις δέ, γέγονας παραβάτης νόμου. Jas. ii. 8–11.

Besides the close parallelism of treatment, the same inversion of the sixth and seventh Commandments is common to both[1]. As previously noted, the distinctive phrase παραβάτης νόμου occurs nowhere else in N.T., except in Rom. ii. 25, 27, while the προσωπολημπτεῖτε is echoed in Rom. ii. 11; and the κατακαυχᾶται which immediately follows (κατακαυχᾶται ἔλεος κρίσεως Jas. ii. 13) is found only in Rom. xi. 18.

Taking all these passages together, it is not too much to say that when Paul was writing to the Romans, the words of our Epistle were fresh in his mind, and came glibly from his pen, and we need not hesitate to regard στρατευομένων ἐν τοῖς μέλεσιν ὑμῶν (Jas. iv. 1) as the precursor of ἐν τοῖς μέλεσίν μου ἀντιστρατευόμενον (Rom. vii. 23), or to overhear in τὸ φρόνημα τῆς σαρκὸς ἔχθρα εἰς θεόν (Rom. viii. 7) an echo from ἡ φιλία τοῦ κόσμου ἔχθρα τοῦ θεοῦ ἐστίν (Jas. iv. 4). On the common use of parallel words, such as ἐλεγχόμενοι, ἔνοχος or ἀποθέσθαι, or even of such a phrase as δικαιοσύνη θεοῦ[2], especially when it occurs in O.T., we may well suspend judgment—they have interest, but as evidence of indebtedness cannot be pressed. In every case priority seems to rest with James; he

[1] The inversion does occur in text B of LXX of Exod. xx. 13, 15, and in Philo, De Decal. 24–5, but cannot be assigned to those sources.

[2] δικαιοσύνη θεοῦ recurs in Rom. i. 16, 17, iii. 21–5 and x. 3, and the contexts in which it occurs tell in favour of derivation from Jas. i. 20. The phrase appears in Micah vi. 5 but only in the sense of justice displayed by God, not in the specific sense of a divine righteousness as contrasted with man's.

is more elementary. Paul appropriates some telling phrase, and sets it off to new advantage; or combines neighbouring expressions into a more trenchant whole; or submits an ethical idea to more searching analysis and scrutiny. To reverse the indebtedness means that James pulled to pieces well-joined clauses, destroyed their balance, dulled their edge, and failed to grasp their deeper implications. And nowhere more glaringly than in his short section upon faith and works.

It may further be observed that, apart from the citations from Genesis and Habakkuk, the Epistle to the Galatians, which traverses so much common ground, shows no correspondences with the Epistle of James like those found in Romans. Inferences from silence are seldom conclusive, but so far as this portion of evidence is concerned, it is reasonable to conclude that in A.D. 48 (adopting the earliest date for Galatians) Paul was not familiar with the Epistle of James, that by A.D. 56 he was; and this would point to publication at some date subsequent to the Council at Jerusalem, between A.D. 49 and 55. In the later Epistles of the Captivity the correspondences in vocabulary nowhere seem decisive.

CHAPTER VIII

CHRISTOLOGY

On Christology proper—the doctrine of the person of Jesus Christ—it seemed well to reserve discussion till the close. The notices in the Epistle are so elementary and undeveloped that implications only are available: and there is no hope of construing these aright, except by aid of the circumstances and aims which determined composition. With their help, examination of the implications becomes fruitful. Of formulated systematic Christology there is none; no scheme of redemption, dependent upon the Incarnation, the Crucifixion or the Resurrection, or on the establishment of saving relations between Christ and the believer, or the risen Christ and God. The author shows no trace of debt to Pauline speculation or modes of presentment; nor yet to the symbolical and transcendental interpretations found in the Epistle to the Hebrews. This is one of the weighty, indeed fatal, objections to assigning a late date to the Epistle: the contrast which it presents in this respect to that of Clement, or the *Didache*, or Hermas is patent and decisive[1].

Explicit mention of Jesus Christ occurs only in the opening salutations of chs. i and ii, and commentators have actually proposed, by the expedient of excision, to refer the Epistle to Jewish, or what may be called pre-Christian authorship[2]. For excision there is not a grain of textual support, and even without the salutations there remain passages scattered about the Epistle in which the Christian implications are express and decisive. Some allowance must be made for an element of intentional reserve, for a desire to refrain from pressing or formulating aspects of belief repugnant to God-fearing Jews. But this consideration does not carry us far; there is no reason to assume or impute the

[1] See further pp. 108, 126.
[2] For criticism of Spitta's proposals, see Mayor pp. clxviii–clxx, and Zahn i. pp. 149–51.

suppression of articles of belief, which to the writer were vital elements in the Christian confession.

Upon these assumptions it is not difficult to apprehend his Christological position: he writes not for an inner circle of disciples, nor yet for gainsaying critics or foes of Judaism, but addresses himself to all devout God-fearing Jews, whose hopes were set upon a spiritual—not a political—regeneration of Israel. He states the case for Christ on the lines of Old Testament teaching and ideals: of incidents in the ministry of Jesus, of signs or wonders, he makes no mention; records no personal impressions, intimacies or disclosures; on the final scenes enacted at Jerusalem he is resolutely, and no doubt deliberately, silent. None of these had formed a part of his first-hand experience, or availed at the time to carry conviction. The claims of Christ, as he presents them, rest on his fulfilment of O.T. ideals, and the soul-satisfying supremacy of his ethical affirmations.

But within these limits, his attitude is not left doubtful. In each salutation (i. 1, ii. 1) Jesus is entitled *Christ*, the Messiah; that affirmation, placed in the forefront of Christian teaching, in itself assigns, in however rudimentary a form, unique values to his person. In both the term of reverence (Lord, *Kurios*) is prefixed; in the expectation of His return (v. 7, 8) it stands alone, sufficient; His is 'the name of honour'[1] which was the patent of their Christian nobility. There is no good reason for referring the expression to the name 'Christians,' which so far as the evidence goes was coined as a term of reproach (A. xi. 26, xxvi. 28, 1 Pet. iv. 16), and was not likely to be thus denoted by James. The sanctification, or profanation, of '*the Name*' was a form of speech familiar to contemporary Judaism[2], and of the deepest religious import: it was constantly associated with the ordeal of martyrdom,

---

[1] καλὸν ὄνομα ii. 7, with which compare A. v. 41–2.

[2] See Foakes Jackson and Lake *Beginnings of Christianity* pp. 63–6. This reference explains the βλασφημοῦσι, which otherwise seems rather unexpected. The τὸ καλὸν ὄνομα τὸ ἐπικληθὲν ἐφ' ὑμᾶς must be derived from Amos ix. 12 ἐφ' οὓς ἐπικέκληται τὸ ὄνομά μου ἐπ' αὐτούς, and it is a noteworthy coincidence that this very verse and phrase is used in the speech of James reported in Acts xv. 13–21, upholding the extension of Christianity to the Gentiles.

or the guilt of apostasy. Nor is it likely that '*the name of honour, by which ye were called*' refers expressly to Baptism; though it denotes in general terms the avowed and consecrated allegiance, the *sacramentum* of fidelity and service owed to Jesus Christ, as liege-lord of conscience and belief.

The *Kurios* designation in itself sheds little light upon exact determination of date. It was an immediate result of the acceptance of the Resurrection[1]; and it is the natural counterpart of the δοῦλος which immediately precedes. It finds a place among the earliest records of the infant Church at Jerusalem[2]: it stands in the forefront of the earliest Epistles of St Paul (Gal. i. 3, 1 Thes. i. 1); and 1 Pet. i. 3 and Jude 4, 17, 21 bear witness to its established place in Judaistic Christendom. So that it can be brought into accord with any date, early or late. But in its company we find a far more specific and unusual term—that of '*the glory*.' No other rendering of ii. 1 seems admissible than '*the faith of our Lord Jesus Christ, the glory*.' 'Faith in the glory' or 'the Lord of glory' are precluded by the order of words. Thus read, the term is highly significant of the *milieu* to which the Epistle belongs. Used thus of a person, a descriptive title of Christ, the term is typically Jewish. The Greek word (δόξα), by derivation and by use, expresses only the human recognition, the ascribed but not the manifested glory, which makes it suitable for the ascription of worship, as in 'Blessing and honour and glory...' (Rev. v. 13, vii. 12, etc.) or 'to whom be honour and glory for ever and ever' (2 Tim. iv. 18, etc.) and its habitual employment in the Pauline Epistles; but utterly inadequate to convey those ideas of the radiance, the lustre, the heavenly sheen, the manifested glory, which clustered round the Jewish doctrine of the Shekinah. The Shekinah idea provides the most typical and vivid symbolism admitted into the severe precincts of Jewish monotheism; in the Burning Bush, on the top of Sinai, in the Holy of Holies, and in many other connexions it finds place, not as a localised presence of the in-

---

[1] On this see Burkitt *Christian Beginnings* pp. 45 ff. In corroboration, compare τὸν μόνον δεσπότην καὶ Κύριον ἡμῶν Ἰησοῦν Χριστόν (Jude 4), the one passage (except the late 2 Pet. ii. 1) in which the term δεσπότης is used of Jesus Christ.

[2] A. ii. 36.

visible God, but as the effect and token of divine action, the visible indication of divine immanence in the phenomenal world. It gives rise to copious varieties of imagery, in which at times—and most of all in the vivid terms of Apocalyptic symbolism[1]—the operative result of the divine activity is hardly distinguished from the divine source from which it proceeds. But the Shekinah idea remained foreign to Greek thought, and, perhaps partly owing to this inadequacy of the term δόξα, in which it was expressed, failed to secure a lodgment in Christian theology. Here and there it lies in the immediate background, as in Rom. ix. 4 'the glory'— that is, the manifestation of the Shekinah—is enumerated among the peculiar privileges of Israel; but otherwise it is confined within the range of Judaistic Christianity[2]. One striking instance is in 1 Pet. iv. 14 'The spirit of the glory, and the spirit of God resteth upon you.' Again, in Heb. ix. 5 'the Cherubim of *Glory* overshadowing the mercy-seat' is drawn direct from the O.T.; but a much more instructive illustration is supplied at the opening of the Epistle, where the Son, 'by whom also he made the ages' is described as 'the effulgence of the glory.'[3] Here, for once, in its appropriate setting, the true Shekinah teaching is enlisted to express the doctrine of the Incarnation: the term 'out-shining' or 'effulgence' of the glory carries its full import, and the Son is regarded not as the reflexion or emanation, but as the actual embodiment—'the out-shining of the glory' in the visible world. As in his person the Creative Word or Wisdom entered into the created order of things, so too he manifested himself as the true effulgence of the divine, the source of emitted light—the 'Light of Light' of the Nicene Creed—in terms which find their more generalised parallel in J. i. 14 'The word became flesh and

[1] E.g. Enoch xiv. 19, 'from underneath the throne came streams of flaming fire..., and the great glory sat thereon'; cf.cii.3,Tobit iii. 16, etc.
[2] In other Pauline passages, such for instance as 'the gospel of the glory of the blessed God,' τὸ εὐαγγέλιον τῆς δόξης τοῦ μακαρίου θεοῦ (1 Tim. i. 11), or τὴν ἐπιφάνειαν τῆς δόξης τοῦ μεγάλου θεοῦ (Tit. ii. 13) the influence of the O.T. use is discernible, and 'the glory' gains by being associated with the revelation of God in Jesus Christ, but in all such passages the idea of 'dignity, honour' suffices to give good sense.
[3] ἀπαύγασμα τῆς δόξης Heb. i. 3.

tabernacled[1] among us, and we beheld *his glory*, the glory as of the only-begotten from the Father.' In our Epistle there is no such developed theology, but the introduction of the term 'the glory,' by its very abruptness in the Greek or English medium, shows how the writer moved instinctively in Jewish categories of thought, and uses language which cannot without violence be attributed to a late date or to Hellenic surroundings. To rest content with the generalised conception—here the identification of the Shekinah with Jesus Christ—is part of the Jewish genius in religion, its capacity for spiritual and intellectual resignation; only under the leadings of Hellenism did Jewish thought feel the need, or even desire, for logical definition, and embark upon the ways of dogmatic exploration.

Another aspect of Christology must be noted, namely the *Parousia* or Coming of Christ. It is present, though not very prominent, in the Epistle, twice introduced as an *ethical motive* for constancy under prolonged trial. '*Be patient, therefore, brethren unto the appearing of the Lord....Stablish your hearts, for the appearing of the Lord is nigh*' (v. 7, 8). The evidence does not justify doctrinaire conclusions. As we should expect of any Judæo-Christian circle, the expectation is still vital, pointing to early date. On the other hand, it is generalised, perhaps rather as a Christian survival of the Messianic expectation so deeply rooted in the hearts of Israel, than as a vivid expectation of the reappearing of a glorified and triumphant Jesus. In Judaistic Christianity the same causes were at work as in Pauline and Hellenic, for gradually reducing the expectation, until with the Fall of Jerusalem it entered upon a new non-Jewish phase. Here it is used not as an incitement to hope, but as an inducement to patience and a justification of pacifism, and the outlook corresponds well with the position of the Church in the middle of the first century. It effectively discountenances late date or Western surroundings.

---

[1] There can be little doubt that the σκηνή, ἐσκήνωσεν terminology is definitely associated with the Hebrew Shekinah. There remains one other passage in N.T., in which ἡ δόξα seems definitely to represent the Shekinah—2 P. i. 17, in which the voice proceeds 'from the magnificent glory,' but this falls later in date and vocabulary.

One other passage, or rather word, invites consideration—'*Ye
have condemned, ye have killed the righteous one*,'[1] which the
R.V. by its rendering definitely refers to the execution of Christ.
But to this there are fatal objections. The phrase of Stephen
in his defence 'Ye denied the Holy and Righteous one' (A. iii. 14)
has been cited in support, but in truth the prefixing of 'the Holy
One' shows that by itself and unsupported 'the righteous' or
'the just' was inadequate as a titular description of Jesus Christ.
The epithet is attached to the name (as in 1 Pet. iii. 18, 1 J. ii. 1),
but except in A. xxii. 14 referring to prophecy, does not stand
alone as a designation: to ears attuned to LXX phraseology, the
established and recurrent use of the term ὁ δίκαιος was generic,
and that would be the assumed meaning[2]. The most familiar
instance, 'The just shall live by faith,' drawn from Habakkuk (and
quoted in Gal., Heb., etc.) is but one of countless instances
scattered up and down the Psalms, Proverbs, Job, Wisdom and
other books[3]. And this generic use alone satisfies the context.
The whole passage is a fervid denunciation of the extortions and
excesses of unbridled wealth, deliberately couched in prophetic
terms. It is the one passage in the Epistle in which the writer
turns openly upon the oppressor, and in so doing falls back upon
Scriptural phraseology. The aorists with which it closes are not
historic, but (like the gnomic aorists, i. 11, 24) aorists of rooted
habitude: '*Ye batten upon the earth, and luxuriate: ye make fat
your hearts in a day of slaughter. Ye pass sentence, ye do to death
the just; he doth not oppose you.*' That at this point the writer
should suddenly fasten upon the persecutors the bygone guilt of
the crucifixion as their crowning offence, runs counter to the
whole handling of the Epistle. He has avoided recriminations
and personalities; remonstrance or reproof has been addressed
almost throughout to his own following; even when adopting the
precepts and even the words of Jesus, he has urged them not on
authority, but upon their own ethical merits. It is conceivable

[1] τὸν δίκαιον v. 6.
[2] So (anarthrously) in v. 16.
[3] δίκαιος and δίκαιοι without article are the more common, but a glance
at the columns of Hatch and Redpath will suffice—e.g. Ps. x. 3, 5,
xxxvi. 12, 16, 21, 26, 32, etc.

that in the background of his mind 'the just' may have included
Jesus, but my own impression is that he would have avoided
rather than welcomed any such ambiguity. And the turn of the
concluding phrase '*He doth not oppose you*' precludes any such
application. The present tense in contrast with the previous
aorists, necessitates a present reference, and cannot refer to action
buried in the past. The word used '*he doth not range himself
against you*'[1] is inappropriate to the death upon the Cross, as
all instances in O.T. or N.T. combine to prove: some other
term, most likely drawn from Messianic prophecy, would have
been chosen. And the ὑμῖν, identifying the present persecutors
with the guilt of their predecessors, has no justification. These
difficulties presumably[2] induced Westcott and Hort to accept the
strained suggestion that the words are a question, and to punctuate
accordingly. The subject to 'Doth not He oppose you?' is supposed to be the Lord of Sabaoth, introduced (as a genitive) in
v. 4. But the objections are decisive. (1) The violent transference
of subject, over-riding the intermediate 'the just' (which immediately precedes) is intolerable, and would never occur to any
reader Greek or English. (2) It would be hard to find a parallel
to so abrupt and unexpected an interrogation, as the finishing
word of remonstrance. If used, it would at least be ushered in
by some particle (οὐχί or another) marking the indignant question.
(3) It breaks up the connexion with the resultant exhortation[3]
'Be patient *therefore*, brethren,...' which Westcott and Hort
space off as a new detached injunction, depriving the οὖν of its
illative value, and missing at a crucial point the author's logic
of appeal. True to his message of patience and endurance, staunch
to his ethical conviction and to Jewish capacity for resignation,
still in the face of persecution and of terrorism he adheres to his
doctrine of non-resistance. '*The righteous doth not resist you.*' It

---

[1] v. 6 οὐκ ἀντιτάσσεται ὑμῖν, LXX uses are but few. The most familiar
is ὁ θεὸς ὑπερηφάνοις ἀντιτάσσεται of Prov. iii. 34, quoted in iv. 6
and repeated 1 P. v. 5. The term denotes a hostile power marshalling
its forces and ranging itself against an adversary, as in the ἀντιτασσόμενος
ἀντιτάξομαι of 1 K. xi. 34, Hos. i. 6.

[2] Hort's invaluable commentary stops short of this point.

[3] Cf. iv. 7, v. 16.

is not for the Christian to oppose violence by violence, to organise revolt, to add one more to the armed factions contending in the name of religion for domination. The passage, alike in protest and in pacifism, is the most fearless and outspoken in the whole Epistle. It may well be that in this paragraph the author issued his own death-warrant. The words would not be forgiven by those whom they denounced. The particular circumstances or occasion of the prosecution and the sentence passed upon James are not recorded: but these words, directly or indirectly, may well have formed part of the count upon which James 'the Just was brought to sentence and done to death,' dying with pardon on his lips (κατεδικάσατε, ἐφονεύσατε τὸν δίκαιον· οὐκ ἀντιτάσσεται ὑμῖν).

CHAPTER IX

RELATION TO OTHER BOOKS—CANONICAL AND SUB-APOSTOLIC

Comparison of our Epistle with other books of the New Testament reflects some light upon the results obtained from internal study. As regards Pauline Epistles, there is little or no evidence beyond that supplied by the Epistle to the Romans, which we have discussed in full[1]. Here and there, in special words such as ἀκαταστασία, the First Epistle to the Corinthians suggests a literary link, but none can be called convincing; and in later Epistles the agreements touch only the ethical vocabulary and add nothing to the evidence of Romans. Thus the one inference is that the Epistle was known to Paul by or before the end of A.D. 55, when he was writing to Rome.

Of the other Epistles two, as attuned to kindred though far from identical conditions of Judaic Christianity, are of especial interest, the First Epistle of St Peter and the Epistle to the Hebrews.

The literary connexion between the Epistle of St James and the First Epistle of St Peter is close and unmistakeable. It is established beyond all gainsaying by the parallel

Jas. i. 2 πᾶσαν χαρὰν ἡγήσασθε... ὅταν πειρασμοῖς περιπέσητε ποικίλοις, γινώσκοντες ὅτι τὸ δοκίμιον ὑμῶν τῆς πίστεως κατεργάζεται ὑπομονήν.

1 P. i. 6 ἐν ᾧ ἀγαλλιᾶσθε, ὀλίγον ἄρτι... λυπηθέντες ἐν ποικίλοις πειρασμοῖς, ἵνα τὸ δοκίμιον ὑμῶν τῆς πίστεως... εὑρεθῇ εἰς ἔπαινον.

This is direct quotation of *unusual* and *distinctive phrases*, and it is confirmed by numerous correspondences scattered throughout the Epistles, though most abundant in the opening chapters of each and affecting the most tell-tale words[2], while of the most

[1] Fully dealt with in Chap. VII.
[2] For parallels see Mayor pp. ci–ciii, compare ἀμίαντος (Jas. i. 27 with 1 P. i. 3), ἄσπιλος (J. i. 27 with 1 P. i. 19), παρακύψαι (J. i. 25 with 1 P. i. 12),

conspicuous[1] O.T. quotations, three are common to both. Thus
there is direct and conscious borrowing, or rather reproduction,
of the most arresting phrases and vocabulary, just those most
fitted to fix themselves in memory. The sole question that arises
is that of *priority*—and there is no reason to dissent from the
conclusion reached by Mayor[2] on careful weighing of the
evidence. Peter fastens on the arresting phrase or epithet, and
refines or embroiders it in his own setting: James' *'crown of
life'* (i. 12) is the germ of Peter's elaborated 'the unfading crown
of glory' (1 P. v. 4), where 'the glory' too has been culled from
Ep. James, and is repeated in 1 P. iv. 14, 'the Spirit of the Glory
and of God.' In the opening quotation, *'beset with temptations
manifold,'* the characteristic postponement of the adjective and
the alliterative beat of the words are sufficient proof that James
provides the original, and the key-words are re-echoed (1 P. iv.
10, 12[3]). In 1 Pet. v. 9 the rather rough 'Whom withstand' (of
the devil) is naturally accounted for by the peremptory, *'Withstand*

ἀνυπόκριτος (J. iii. 17 with 1 P. i. 22) and ἀπροσωπολήμπτως 1 P. i. 17 with
Jas. ii. 1 μὴ ἐν προσωπολημψίαις; and also the phrases

τὸν στέφανον τῆς ζωῆς J. i. 12.

τὸν ἀμαράντινον τῆς δόξης στέφανον 1 P. v. 4

ἀντίστητε τῷ διαβόλῳ J. iv. 7.

ὁ ἀντίδικος διάβολος..., ᾧ ἀντίστητε 1 P. v. 8, 9.

ταπεινώθητε ἐνώπιον Κυρίου καὶ
ὑψώσει ὑμᾶς J. iv. 10.

ταπεινώθητε οὖν ὑπὸ τὴν κραταιὰν
χεῖρα τοῦ θεοῦ ἵνα ὑμᾶς ὑψώσῃ
1 P. v. 6.

ἀποθέμενοι περισσείαν κακίας
J. i. 21.

ἀποθέμενοι πᾶσαν κακίαν 1 P. ii. 1.

ἐκ τῶν ἡδονῶν ὑμῶν τῶν στρατευομένων...ἐπιθυμεῖτε J. iv. 1.

τῶν σαρκικῶν ἐπιθυμιῶν αἵτινες
στρατεύονται 1 P. ii. 11.

[1] Is. xl. 7 πᾶσα σὰρξ χόρτος καὶ πᾶσα δόξα ἀνθρώπου ὡς ἄνθος χόρτου·
ἐξηράνθη ὁ χόρτος καὶ τὸ ἄνθος ἐξέπεσεν is common to Jas. i. 11 and 1 P. i. 24.
Jas. v. 20 καλύψει πλῆθος ἁμαρτιῶν recurs verbatim 1 P. iv. 8, and is
the more remarkable, as derived from the Hebrew, while LXX reads
πάντας τοὺς μὴ φιλονεικοῦντας καλύπτει Prov. x. 12. The κύριος ὑπερηφάνοις ἀντιτάσσεται ταπεινοῖς δὲ δίδωσι χάριν of Prov. iii. 34 appears in
Jas. iv. 6 and 1 P. v. 5, and again the two agree in the slight variant ὁ θεός
for the κύριος of LXX; the words that immediately follow are also
echoes from James.
[2] Mayor *Ep. St James* pp. xcviii f., cxxxviii f.; Zahn 1. 133–4 and
Blenkin *Ep. St Peter* in Camb. Gk. T., pp. lv–lx give a careful study of
the parallels. [3] 1 P. iv. 10 καλοὶ οἰκονόμοι ποικίλης χάριτος θεοῦ.

the devil' of St James iv. 7, where the preservation of mood and tense is in itself telling; without St James in his mind St Peter would have surely written ἀνθίστασθε: the *aorist*, one of a long series[1], is in the characteristic manner of St James, as in πᾶσαν χαρὰν ἡγήσασθε (i. 2), and a number of instances in chs. iv and v.

Quotation of the kind here used has more than literary interest: it is no mere measure of individual indebtedness, but it is quotation addressed to the readers, in the same kind of way as citation of Scripture in sermons, and carries with it inferences not without value. St Peter, writing to the Jewish Dispersion in Asia Minor, uses catchwords and echoes from St James as invested with association and appeal: and these would have special poignancy if the Epistle was written shortly after James' violent death in A.D. 62. In other words, Peter pays tribute to the position of personal influence and authority which James held at Jerusalem. St Peter's own association with the mother Church comes to an end, so far as N.T. records serve, with his withdrawal after arrest and imprisonment by Herod in A.D. 42. From that point James takes possession, and the traditions, however uncertain and conflicting, agree in placing the scene of St Peter's activities elsewhere, while according to Eusebius[2], Clement of Alexandria expressly stated that Peter and John combined in preferring James the Just to the headship of the Church in Jerusalem. Among Peter's subsequent activities none is better attested than that official connexion with Antioch which has the endorsement of Origen, Ignatius, Eusebius and Jerome; this would give natural links with Syrian[3] Christians on the one hand, and on the other with Asiatic Churches, addressed in his Epistle. There the opening salutation is modelled on St James' precedent, though 'the Dispersion' is applied in its specific geographical sense to the 'sojourners in Pontus, Galatia, Cappadocia, Asia and Bithynia,' that is, to Jews of Asia Minor. And to those of his

[1] E.g. ὑποτάγητε, ἀντίστητε, ἐγγίσατε, καθαρίσατε, ἁγνίσατε and several more (Jas. iv. 7–8).

[2] *H. E.* ii. i. 3.

[3] Edmundson *The Church in Rome* pp. 50, 77. In the Clementine literature Syria is throughout the scene of the pre-Roman encounters between Peter and Simon Magus. See pp. 133–7.

readers who could connect them with James, the quotations selected are well adapted to wake active chords of remembrance.

From the purely literary side the question of priority does not to my mind admit of doubt. But from the side of content and context it becomes clearer still. Any attempt to reverse the connexion entails objections far graver than those of literary handling. In 1 P. i. 3–7 the palmary quotation is embedded in triumphant affirmations of belief in the victorious and redeeming powers of the revealed and risen Christ. Isolation from their context comes near to repudiation of its content. It is hard to imagine or reconstruct conditions under which a Christian writer, whether of the first or second century, could have detached and quoted these subordinated words, and fallen back upon the lower levels of the inchoate Christology associated with them in our Epistle. In their own setting, addressed to readers tried and sore bested, they make a fine and forcible appeal; but as extracts from a far richer environment of 'living and exalted hope' they are robbed of all their inspiration. They stand denuded of motive-power and recompense, and become a half-hearted echo, which shrinks from any vital belief in the Gospel of the Resurrection, a reversion from the Christian hope to the levels of Old Testament agnosticism, from St Peter to the son of Sirach. Up to a point, for instance in the Jewish thought of God and of 'the glory' (1 P. i. 21, iv. 13–14, v. 1, etc.), in the appreciation of 'faith' (1 P. i. 7, 9) and of 'temptation,' in the emphasis on conduct, in the appeal to Old Testament Scriptures and their use in citation, in the acceptance of Jesus as the Christ (1 P. i. 3–13, iii. 15, etc.) with the expectation of a near return to judgment (1 P. iv. 7), in the identification of Christian believers with the true Israel (1 P. i. 1, ii. 9), the two writers are close akin; but the Epistle of Peter passing beyond these substructures of Judaic thought, and also of personal reminiscence, shows the impress of Hellenic surroundings, and also of Pauline thought and teaching (especially as embodied in the Epistle to the Romans[1]) upon the meaning and person of Christ—not only is Jesus the Teacher and the Pattern (1 P. ii. 21), the Chief Shepherd and the Overseer of Souls (1 P. ii. 25, v. 4),

[1] See Blenkin's edition *Ep. St Peter* in Camb. Gk. Test. pp. lx–lxiv.

but the Crucifixion and the Resurrection both enter upon new categories of spiritual meaning. New values representative, sacrificial (i. 19) and redemptive, are attached to the death upon the Cross, in its efficacy for the forgiveness of sins and the communication of righteousness (ii. 24, iii. 18, iv. 18), and the Rising again is not only the vindication of holiness and the reversal of earthly humiliation (i. 11, iv. 13, v. 1), but also the assumption into eternal or even co-equal glory with the divine (i. 11, iii. 22). The assumption that the author of the Epistle, with that of Peter under his eyes and borrowing from it words and phrases and quotations, ignored or turned his back upon the whole of this advance, denies to him all capacity of spiritual insight, and even, unless some fanciful environment is invented, of ethical force or virtue. Affirmations which at Jerusalem faced and met the risk of martyrdom, if transferred to Asia or Italy, are reduced to the irresponsible utterances of an anonymous pamphleteer. As such they become of little moment, open to the charge of being even on the ethical side no more than an 'epistle of straw.'

It seems needless to consider verbal parallels in the Second Epistle, assuming it to be of late date and by another hand.

The Epistle to the Hebrews shows no links of literary[1] obligation, beyond those which rest on partial similarity of circumstance, or on common backgrounds of religious belief. Under the latter may be included the appeal to Old Testament Scriptures as authoritative[2], even though methods of interpretation diverge so widely, the association of Shekinah thought with the person of Jesus[3], and the stress laid upon operative 'faith'[4] as cardinal in the Jewish apprehension of God: under the former, the reiterated call to endurance and to stedfastness in face of bitter social and religious persecution, and the expectation of the approaching End[5]. Detailed study of comparisons or contrasts would require

---

[1] Unless it be found in the association of νεκρά with πίστις and ἔργα, which is peculiar to these two Epistles—Jas. ii. 17, 26, Heb. vi. 1, ix. 14; but more or less close resemblances occur; v. Westcott on Heb. vi. 1.

[2] Heb. i. 1. [3] Heb. i. 3. [4] Heb. vi. 1, 12 and xi.

[5] For prominence of ὑπομονή compare Jas. i. 4, 12, v. 11 and Heb. x. 32, 36, xii. 1, 7, etc.; for notes of persecution Heb. x. 32-4, xii. 3 ff., xiii. 3; for expectation of the Parousia Heb. iii. 7, 13, x. 25.

a separate treatise, and carry us into planes of thought entirely foreign to St James. Suffice it to say that if, as seems far most probable[1], the Epistle to the Hebrews was addressed to some circle of Syrian or Palestinian believers under the shadow of the Jewish War, it shows from its own angle of vision how swiftly and surely after the judicial murder of James events moved to their inevitable end. The rift which James vainly hoped to heal or to surmount had proved intractable: already the avalanche was in motion, and the final cleavage was at hand. The issues between Christ and Judaism lay deeper than any ethical concordat; in Him the system of Judaism was found wanting, its modes and provisions 'antiquated, obsolete and doomed to vanish,'[2] no longer adequate to the spiritual needs of men. Judaism might, if it would, have assimilated the ethic of Jesus, but was irreconcileable with the deeper understanding of His Person; living and dying he had 'inaugurated a new and living way.'[3]

Akin, in some respects, to the Epistle to the Hebrews, the Epistle of Barnabas is the product of a more fanciful and bookish school of typology, and represents Alexandrian, not Palestinian, currents of thought. Whatever be the actual date, it is subsequent to the fall of Jerusalem, and even apart from the more pronounced Christology shows no conclusive contacts with the Epistle of St James. The few verbal correspondences discoverable do not suggest literary obligation[4].

As regards the Synoptic Gospels, there are no marks of specific relationship with Mark or Luke[5]. The Marcan narrative contains (vi. 13) a mention of the disciples anointing with oil, but the parallel injunction in Jas. v. 14 seems to refer definitely to the practice of the synagogue, and suggests no claim to Christian precedent. The affinities are all with Matthew, derived that is to say from the same stratum of tradition, as that from which the

---

[1] The attempt to refer it to Rome, at some vaguely later date, seems to me a freakish paradox that ignores plain historic implications.
[2] Heb. viii. 13 τὸ παλαιούμενον καὶ γηράσκον ἐγγὺς ἀφανισμοῦ.
[3] Heb. x. 20 ἐνεκαίνισεν ἡμῖν ὁδὸν πρόσφατον καὶ ζῶσαν.
[4] Mayor p. liv.   [5] Knowling p. xxii.

Gospel according to Matthew drew; but—with the exception of
v. 12 which has already been discussed at length—detailed
examination shows how fluid and variable was the form as yet
attained[1]. Considering how much ground is common to the
Epistle and to the Sermon on the Mount, the noticeable feature
is the *absence* of verbal agreement: parallel precepts, principles
and axioms are expressed in language varying in terms, and
dependent on a tradition not yet fixed or stereotyped. The one
inference to be drawn from such divergences is that of early
date. Even if the Gospels of Mark and Luke belong to other
spheres of influence, the publication of that according to Matthew
must have produced traces of literary dependence such as are
plentiful in Clement, Barnabas, the *Didache*, Ignatius and
others[2]. Into the debt of these sub-Apostolic writers to James
we need not go closely; in substance it is inconsiderable, and its
interest lies chiefly in the lexical direction. Literary connexion
between James and Clement of Rome seems clear, and hardly
less so that James is the earlier. Clement is a born quoter, with
little originative gift: ταπεινοφροσύνη and ἀκαταστασία he may
well have derived from Paul, but the combination ἐν ἀλαζονείᾳ
καὶ ἀκαταστασίᾳ (c. 14) is reminiscent of James: note the tell-tale
ἐν, and ἐγκαυχώμενοι ἐν ἀλαζονείᾳ αὐτῶν (c. 21) compared with
καυχᾶσθε ἐν ταῖς ἀλαζονείαις ὑμῶν (iv. 16) is too much for mere
coincidence. Nor would διψυχεῖν and διψυχία find vogue, until
δίψυχος had led the way. Those who put James after Hermas
seem impervious to literary reasonings[3]: for the most outstanding
parallels see Mayor pp. lviii–lxii, and Westcott *Canon· of New
Testament* p. 198.

[1] See pp. 67–8.
[2] For parallels see Mayor pp. lii ff.
[3] See Moffatt, p. 467; Harnack and Ropes, pp. 88–90, deny literary
dependence.

CHAPTER X

LATE AUTHORSHIP AND DATE

So far the internal, and the literary, inferences fall into natural, and to my mind convincing accord. But it remains true that many writers of learning and repute have rejected this conclusion, and for one reason or another adopt rival alternatives. Dissent in many cases took its start from the mistaken assumption that James was controverting the antinomian teaching of St Paul, and Tubingen contentions of a standing feud between Paul and Peter (with his Jerusalem associates), did much to colour the views of commentators: for that reason I have dealt at length with that particular issue. But if once early date is abandoned, and the Epistle of St James is regarded as posterior to the Pauline and the Petrine Epistles, all firm standing ground is cut away and (as might be expected) date and provenance become purely conjectural, and the more they can be put out of touch with any known historical surroundings, the more freedom is gained for fancy combinations.

Avoiding side issues and debate I have tried to realise and reconstruct the historical surroundings and atmosphere in which the Epistle came to birth; and so to consolidate a constructive position and presentment, which is the best defence against more or less random and desultory attacks: but in a field like this, merely to ignore objections and alternatives may seem shirking or disingenuous. Against a clear-cut issue, posed as a positive and constructive alternative, argument would be simple. But there is hardly a problem of New Testament criticism in which there is less agreement, or approach to agreement. Some[1], upholding the authorship of James, assign composition to the last year or so of his life (*c.* A.D. 61), and claim priority for the Epistles of Paul (except the Pastoral), and even (though the strain is violent) for 1 Peter: others favour *indirect* attribution to James, regarding

[1] Moffatt *Introd. N.T.* p.470, gives leading references, and casts his own vote in favour of the first quarter of the second century. But in many cases judgments are little more than incidental, and open to revision.

the Epistle as notes of an address, or as compiled from *Logia*, uttered in Aramaic, but invested with Greek dress by some follower or secretary or scribe, perhaps in tribute to his memory. Among those who place it after the Jewish War, some associate it with Judæo-Christian circles in Syria or Cilicia, others with Gentile Churches in Asia or the West: some connect it with the period and school of Clement of Rome (A.D. 96), some with the more vague and relaxed Christianity of Hermas, or even relegate it (with Harnack) to the latter part of the second century. And it is hardly possible to say which theory can claim the more influential names in its support. The collision of judgments is complete, and few look upon the subject whole; too often some isolated analogy, or some piecemeal objection, is allowed to determine the choice. The detached injunction about oaths, for instance, is treated as evidence of Essene or Ebionite affinities. But in the Epistle taken as a whole there is no hint of the lustrations and ablutions, of the common meals and the ascetic regimen, which played so prominent a part in their systems; in Ebionite writing James himself administered oaths of terrifying solemnity; and an Ebionite writer is one of the last who would have introduced his author as simple and untitled 'James.' The weight of evidence is decisive for another source. Others seize on a single obscure and baffling phrase (iii. 6) and assume some late Orphic or neo-Platonic lineage, without regard to all that makes against it.

Within reasonable compass it is only possible to single out and define the crucial points, which must be applied as tests to the particular solution offered. As regards historic setting, the Judaic cast and background of the whole is beyond question; and the more closely the Epistle is scrutinised, the more fundamental and pervading does it appear to be; it is no mere question of reference or quotation; while much in the outer dress and trimmings is Greek, the heart of the thought and the expression is Hebraic. The Jewish scriptures are the fountain of authority and inspiration; and 'the witness of Jesus is the spirit of prophecy.'

Comparison with sub-Apostolic writings such as those ascribed to Clement (himself perhaps a Jew) reveals thin and obvious resemblances; and it is easy to enumerate defects shared in common; but the contrasts are far more telling, and to those who know the ground, attempts to bring the Epistle of James into line with Clement of Rome, or the *Shepherd*, or the *Didache*, can only issue in discomfiture. They have moved out of the Jewish enclosure. Apart from ethical moments which may be reserved for later discussion, their relations to Church order and institutional developments, to literature sacred and profane, to the surrounding world of heathenism and of rival mythologies and cultures, their attitude to current Christological beliefs and teaching, consign them to a different class and *milieu*, as distinctive as that which belongs to the Epistle of Barnabas or to that to Diognetus. The phœnix of Clement, the eucharistic ritual of the *Didache*[1], the Perseus or Hermes analogies of Justin[2], are as foreign to our Epistle as is the classification of idol forms— bronze, marble, silver or terra-cotta[3]—or the animal typology[4], which appears in the pages of the Alexandrines. To the casual reader, the absence of topical and personal references may seem to deprive the Epistle of distinctive feature and physiognomy. This is usually the case where an ethical appeal is generalised, as for instance in many of the Minor Prophets, or in such imperishable works as the *Encheiridion*, or the *De Imitatione*. But here, as there, the setting and the scene is implied with perfect clearness. There emerges the picture of a community, or rather a complex of communities, exposed to hardships, threats and social disabilities for conscience sake, cleaving to the Scripture promises while claiming the Christian franchise, beset with sectarian jealousies and strife of tongues, finding their vent in acts of official violence or of overt war, and themselves tempted continually to let material and worldly interests prevail over the dictates of spiritual conviction and the fear of God. Where is it possible to find objective realities corresponding to the picture except in Palestine, and above all in Jerusalem, during the years antecedent to the Jewish War?

This is the issue which destructive criticism has to face.

The opening salutation is a case in point. From the positive

[1] *Did*. §§ 9–10.
[2] Just. M. 1 *Apol*. xxi. xxii.
[3] *Ep. Diogn*. §§ 2.
[4] Barnabas §§ 8, 10.

side we have seen how congruous and apposite it is to the exceptional position held by James at Jerusalem[1]: on the other hand, to upholders of pseudonymous authorship of late date it presents obstacles, which it may be easy to ignore but difficult to surmount or circumvent. If 'James' is a *pseudonym* for James of Jerusalem, how comes it that no title of authority, no institutional claim of any kind, and no substantive allusion is anywhere introduced? that no apparent purpose, beyond that of ethical appeal, can be detected? Still further, upon the attendant assumption that James left nothing behind him in writing, would any one who sought a hearing have hoped to secure it, or have got it, under cover of his name? 'James' would in that case tend rather to discredit, than to establish, Apostolic authorship. A *second* Epistle of Peter, a *second* or *third* of John, a feigned Epistle or Epistles of Paul, are not unnatural phenomena, and the name might have carried weight or helped acceptance; but an Epistle of James could hardly have failed to raise doubts and questionings, until the day of those later Apocrypha and Acts, which never fail to reveal their aim and *raison d'être*. In this class of literature, naturally enough, epistles have little part; they are a difficult and risky form of composition to simulate and to palm off as genuine[2].

Others suggest that the name is no pseudonym, but that the Epistle was written—as was said of the Homeric poems—by 'some other fellow of the same name.' When, where, and in what surroundings did he live? and how came he to imagine that mere coincidence of name invested him with the cloak of prophetic, or even Apostolic, authority? By what title did he summon '*the twelve Tribes which are in Dispersion*' to give ear to his message? Through what channels did he propose to gain access to them, or elicit intelligible response? This part of the salutation becomes a very serious difficulty. How is it compatible with a date subsequent to the destruction of Jerusalem? The term Dispersion came into currency as a natural counterpart to Jeru-

---

[1] Cf. pp. 12, 15, 19.

[2] From the Epistles of Phalaris to those of Shakespeare by W. H. Ireland, the forger has rarely if ever succeeded in covering his traces.

salem regarded as the theocratic centre of a racial faith. It embodied the instinct of hereditary unity based on common belief, and owing allegiance to a central sanctuary and religious organisation. With the destruction of the Temple, the extirpation of the hierarchy, and the final razing of Jerusalem, the term died a natural death, except for historic or symbolic purposes: all Jewry was 'in Dispersion'; and the unity of Israel was sufficiently denoted by 'the Jews,' which in the Apologists, the letter to Diognetus, and in Christian literature generally, becomes habitual. And the later the date assigned, the more formidable becomes the difficulty.

Some resort to the simple expedient of excision, and Harnack surmises that the opening verse was prefixed, towards the end of the second century, to a collection of sayings compiled some fifty years earlier (A.D. 120–150), possibly by followers of James. It might be enough to reply that no single manuscript or version supports such Gordian treatment, and to urge that blank rejection of evidence is a capital offence in historic criticism. But, apart from this, excision does not help; early or late, the verse is there and has to be accounted for, and no arbitrary post-dating removes or lessens the difficulties of explanation. To hit upon these terms, alike in what they contain and in what they withhold, required a very subtle impersonator, whom no lapse of time would help. And it is too much to suppose that a late prescript, prefixed to a nameless document current in the West, secured from Syriac churches and from Origen an attribution to James of Jerusalem, and therewith eventual canonicity!

Next, for the links of literary association. Detailed examination has led us to the conclusion that the Epistle was antecedent to the Epistle to the Romans and 1 Peter. Those who reverse the relation have to maintain that the author was familiar with and utilised the writings of both Apostles, but that he tacitly disclaimed, or at least betrays no consciousness of, the Christological doctrines by which they set most store: that he was intimate with the words and teaching of Jesus, but had no acquaintance with the Synoptic record: that of Johannine thought he shows no trace, and equally no taint of Gnostic or of Ebionite speculations. How difficult it is to reconcile such data will be obvious at once; and to examine the possible combinations a thankless and unprofitable task. Every theory will have its own dilemmas to face: but in such a case, it behoves the higher critic, so far as he is a searcher after constructive truth, to define and test his own position, to make sure of what is tenable, and not to accept the mere paralysis of incongruous hypotheses.

Nowhere is the issue more direct than in the field of Christology. Either the Epistle presents us with an '*inchoate*,' or else with a '*blanched*' theology[1]. Traditional and early authorship implies that James, while pleading the paramount claims of the ethical teaching of Jesus, had either not yet come to attach to the person of 'the Lord Jesus Christ' as manifested in the flesh the attributes and the theological implications, which within his own lifetime became integral parts and verities of Christian belief, or else that in this Epistle he deliberately held them in reserve as of subordinate importance for the purpose which he had in view. On the assumption of later date, the authorship of James, and (in most cases) association with Jerusalem, is dismissed: the Epistle is taken to represent the more relaxed and undogmatic Christianity, which followed as a reaction from the creative force and originality of Paul, and which, while not repudiating his doctrines of sin, atonement, redemption and grace, chose rather in the hands of moralists, allegorists and apologists (such as the author of 2 Clem., Hermas and Justin Martyr) to come to terms with the theistic beliefs, the philosophic morality, and even the mythology of enlightened Paganism. The Epistle goes even further in avoiding all reference to the death or resurrection of Jesus, or to the ordinances of Christian worship, and is interpreted as an evidence of the waning power of Pauline or Johannine speculation, and the reduction of Christianity to ethical rather than theological beliefs—in a word, it is the product of spiritual decadence. The difficulty is to reconcile this temper either with the Hebraic setting and assumptions that dominate the whole, or with the prophetic tension and glow with which they are

---

[1] The phrase is from Moffatt *Lit. N.T.* 471, and its pungency has been recognised by Kennedy.

applied. The Hebraic and Hellenic tempers do not blend easily, and at this period the way of fusion was chiefly found through allegorical or Gnostic media, of which the Epistle shows no trace. In truth, transferred to this surrounding, the Epistle does not shed a ray of new light from any quarter or in any direction, but is merely denuded of all that is characteristic and instructive.

Regarded as a compilation from recorded utterances, the literary phenomena and associations become inexplicable, and the sayings themselves, disengaged from the personal setting and occasions which brought them into being, retain little value. On the other hand, assuming it to be the production of a later and unplaced pseudonymous writer, the Epistle becomes the work of one who, while borrowing phrases from 1 Pet. i. 6–7 (and other passages), deliberately cancelled all reference to the Christian hope and belief in which they lay embedded, and in exchange for the Resurrection message and 'the living hope' of Peter falls back upon the Old Testament moralities of the son of Sirach; in his approach to Pauline doctrines, he shows himself incapable of understanding, much less of sharing or assimilating, the spiritual experiences and intuitions on which Paul based his interpretation of the Incarnation and his attitude to Judaism; he reverts to bygone forms and methods of prophetic appeal, to a belated renewal of controversies that had passed, and to a denunciation of feuds and factions that lay silenced in the grave. It is hard to reconcile this reactionary outlook with the phenomena and characteristics of the literary style; harder still to find a niche for such a writer in any known post-Apostolic surrounding; and perhaps hardest of all to understand how a production of the kind could—on the mere strength of a pseudonym—gain attentive hearing and eventually attain to canonicity.

CHAPTER XI

THE CHURCH AT JERUSALEM, UNDER THE LEADERSHIP OF JAMES

Ethical values depend upon the surroundings which bring them into play, and it is therefore essential before attempting a final estimate of the values of the Epistle, regarded as a message of James to the early Church of Jerusalem, to realise the fortunes and circumstances of the Church itself[1]. The imprisonment of Peter and his consequent withdrawal took place in A.D. 42, the execution of James in A.D. 62. Every age is in some sense an age of transition: but of no era is that more sensationally true than of these twenty years, which are associated with the leadership of James. The mere length of his tenure is a tribute to his capacity; but much more, when we realise the ordeals and crises which it had to encounter. For these years set the seal to two of the most momentous decisions in the history of world-religion. (1) They endorsed the final rejection of Jesus by the Jewish people. 'It was necessary,' said Paul and Barnabas to the Jews of Antioch, 'that the word of God should first be spoken to you: seeing that ye thrust it from you, and judge yourselves unworthy of eternal life, lo *we turn to the Gentiles*' (A. xiii. 46). And the official leaders at Jerusalem ratified the new departure. In the sequel it meant the liberation of Western monotheism from the codes of Israel; and a sentence of excommunication inflicted on the chosen people by themselves. (2) The same years sealed the forfeiture of Jewish nationality. An implacable and suicidal nationalism threw down the challenge to Rome, and in the name of patriotism provoked against itself the ban that forfeited all rights of nationality. It is perhaps no exaggeration to say that the judicial murder of James preluded both issues—the final rupture with the Christians, and the fight to a finish with Imperial Rome. It was the ultimatum of racial bigotry to the religion of personal piety.

[1] The position up to departure of Peter has been outlined in Chapter III.

In previous pages we surveyed the conditions that prevailed in Northern Palestine during the lifetime of Jesus: the year of Crucifixion, in which James joined the Christian community at Jerusalem, marks also the beginnings of disruption. The death of Philip the Tetrarch in A.D. 34, the banishment of Herod Antipas in A.D. 37, and the supersession of Pontius Pilate as procurator of Judæa in A.D. 36 were steps in the process of disintegration. In A.D. 37 the strong hand of Tiberius was removed, and the sacrilegious pretensions of Caligula did much to exasperate religious bitterness. Alike in the line of Procurators and of High Priests, all settled continuity disappears from the administration of Judæa. If for a moment the consolidation of power in the hands of Herod Agrippa I (A.D. 41) held out a fleeting promise of Judaic unity, his catastrophic death in A.D. 44 sounded its last knell under the primacy of Rome. His son and heir, a youth of seventeen, was detained at Rome, and for years not allowed to enter on even a small part of his ancestral inheritance. Judæa was once more placed under Procuratorial control, but successive minions of the 'pumpkin' Claudius brought nothing but discredit on the name of Rome. With insufficient forces, entangled in intrigues imperial and local, domestic and personal, their brief tenures of authority were but an uneasy scramble to keep themselves in the saddle, and to line their pockets with the gains of office. Brigandage and sedition became chronic, a result partly of political and racial jealousies, but more often of religious feuds and fanaticism, exacerbated by Pharisaic intransigents in Galilee and the provinces, and at Jerusalem by the Sadducean intrigues of the high-priests of the Annas clan[1]. Such is the background of national decomposition, amid which James 'upheld the Christ,' and in the light of which his Epistle must be judged. The doings and the records of the time are such hotbeds of personal scandal and recrimination, that it is hard to frame broad conclusions, and

---

[1] Klausner *Jesus of Nazareth* Bk. II, p. 129 ff. (cf. p. 222), gives a good summary of the Zealot risings and outbreaks, extracted from the pages of Josephus, but how is it possible to reconcile such records of wholesale massacre and pillage with the pictures of prosperity and wealth and population which he elsewhere ascribes to the same regions?

the pages of Josephus give little help towards estimating the exact part played by James and his followers.

The first Procurator, Cuspius Fadus (A.D. 44–46), had to deal with the abortive rising of Theudas, the false prophet, in Judæa. His successor Tiberius Alexander, A.D. 46–48, with the more formidable revolt of Judas and his sons in Galilee. During his *biennium* occurred the fatal promotion of Ananias to the High-priesthood, which he was destined to occupy for twelve disastrous years (A.D. 47–59). He had entered upon office when Paul and Barnabas came to the conference at Jerusalem (A.D. 48), and later in Acts xxiii. 2–xxiv. 1 reappears as prosecutor of St Paul. He was a bitter and rapacious partisan, whose greed and violence paved the way for the final catastrophe. In A.D. 48 Cumanus took charge in place of Tiberius Alexander, and at the following Passover occurred the sanguinary tumult in the Temple, to which Josephus attributes a death-roll of not less than 20,000[1]. A little later, in retaliation for assaults upon Galilæan pilgrims, the Jews of Jerusalem raided the Samaritan territory, and Cumanus was compelled to place his military forces in the field[2]. Things were on the verge of civil war; the Prefect of Syria, Ummidius Quadratus, was compelled to intervene in person. The Samaritans appealed to Rome, with the result that Cumanus and Ananias were both remanded to the bar of the Emperor. There Ananias deftly won the ear of Agrippina, the consort of Claudius; and under her influence Cumanus was banished, his tribune publicly disgraced and executed, and Ananias resumed his sway in Jerusalem, while Felix, brother to the freedman favourite Pallas, became his Excellency in the Procuratorship (A.D. 52)[3]. Under such conditions not only minorities and suspects, but all defence-less and law-abiding citizens became liable to the same kind of legalised extortion as ecclesiastical corporations and commissaries were able to inflict say in the fourteenth or fifteenth centuries of English history, but far more savage in its methods. How chronic

---

[1] Jos. *Ant.* xx. v; *B. J.* II. xii.
[2] Jos. *Ant.* xx. vi; Tac. *Ann.* XII. 54 '*arsisset bello provincia.*'
[3] Acts xxiii. 26 τῷ κρατίστῳ ἡγεμόνι Φήλικι, and xxiv. 3 κράτιστε Φῆλιξ. Cf. *Ant.* xx. vii.

and severe their sufferings were, may be inferred from the
organised collections made 'for the poor saints at Jerusalem'
throughout the churches of the West: during the two years (or
more) preceding Paul's last journey to Jerusalem these were
maintained assiduously. The distress has been attributed to rash
experiments in Christian communism; but the assumption is
gratuitous, and it is quite unlikely that churches of Galatia and
Ephesus, of Macedonia and Achaia, would have combined to
subsidise destitution produced in that way. Rather, it was the
inevitable outcome of misrule, and of the situation reflected in
our Epistle.

And further inferences of interest may be drawn. The collection
is evidence of the close contact maintained between the Christians
of Jerusalem and those of the Dispersion: and the main channel
of communication must have been through Jews and Jewish
Christians going to and fro to the yearly feasts. Paul and his
companions themselves furnish an instance; their time-table was
regulated by his desire to reach Jerusalem in time for Pentecost.
The appointment and choice of emissaries is evidence how coherent and influential the Christian community at Jerusalem
continued to be. The list supplied in Acts[1] consists of honoured
names from leading churches; they would not have gone up as
official representatives except to a church with recognised status
and effective organisation. The arrival of the delegation falls a
year or two later than that to which literary indications point
as the date of composition. Things were going from bad to worse,
but without substantial change in the situation. The breach with
Judaism was not yet declared, nor even as it seemed inevitable.
That position is still openly maintained, and without contradiction, by Paul himself in his defence addressed to Felix, A.D. 55,
an expert in such matters (A. xxiv. 10 ff.). The πόλεμοι καὶ μάχαι
(iv. 1) have reference to the outbreaks perpetrated in Samaria,
and reproduced in Galilee[2]. The greed of Ananias and his

---

[1] A. xx. 4, with Paul and Luke in addition.

[2] Cf. Tac. *Ann.* xii. 54, and see p. 30 n. Between πόλεμοι καὶ μάχαι
(iv. 1) and the μάχεσθε καὶ πολεμεῖτε of iv. 2 come φονεύετε καὶ ζηλοῦτε.
Every Greek reader must feel the curious weakness of ζηλοῦτε; E.V.

R 8

associates had become a crying scandal (v. 1–6) and its consequences were spreading ruin over the whole country-side (v. 4). James had already presided for seven years or more over the Church at Jerusalem, and at this critical interlude (A.D. 51) devout and peace-loving Jews (iii. 18) of whatever following— Christian or Pharisee—would look to him for some word of guidance and support, under the growing reign of terror fomented by the Nationalists, who were already banding themselves into armed groups of Zealots and Dagger-Men (*Sicarii*)[1].

A setting such as this brings into relief the moral breadth and dignity, the combination of outspokenness and self-restraint, which inspire and animate the whole. It is a call to the true Israel, to all forces of righteousness and of good will, to redress their promised heritage. In the name of Jesus Christ, as Servant of the one God, James bids them put aside the spirit of disaffection and of hate, of sectarianism and pride, and through the royal law of love attain the perfect way of liberty. He abstains from any word that can accentuate disputed issues, or provoke the spirit of controversy[2]. However sorely tried, let them remember that trials, afflictions, deprivations are God's appointed school of endurance, patience and humility. He adjusts his emphasis to the needs that were most vital: his sternest denunciations are for the misuse of privilege and wealth and power; for the healing of the spirit of revolt and schism, the one antidote is strict bridling of the tongue and of the temper of censoriousness: in that let

revisers have changed the rendering from 'desire to have' to 'covet.' But ζηλοῦτε is not the word of the Tenth Commandment. If only we associate it with the 'Zealots,' who were more and more becoming a distinctive faction, the word at once gains apt and proper force, and carries with it the ζῆλον of iii. 14. Lightley's study of the Zealots in *Jewish Sects and Parties* pp. 327 ff. amply justifies such specific reference. See also Klausner *Jesus of Nazareth* pp. 203–5.

[1] In the pages of Josephus the *Sicarii* first appear under the regime of Felix, who seems himself to have instigated the assassination of the ex-Highpriest Jonathan, in the Temple precincts, at their hands. *Ant.* xx. viii. 5–10.

[2] Kent pp. 284–6 emphasises these points, and describes the Epistle as 'a strong and noble homily,' but robs them of virtue by relegating them to some unknown context of the second century.

none offend. For the kingdom of righteousness, mercy and loving-kindness are of more avail than any outward observance or profession. Only through prayer and stedfast waiting upon God can men regain the '*Wisdom that is from above, and the fruit of peace for them that make peace*' (iii. 18).

Felix was still in power when Paul resolved upon that final visit to Jerusalem, which the divine voice inflexibly imposed upon him (A. xx. 23, xxi. 13, 14). James realised better than he the risks which it entailed, and on his arrival, in time for the Pentecostal celebrations, proposed a plan which might, he hoped, avert disaster (A. xxi. 22). Paul's unhesitating compliance shows the length he was prepared to go in co-operation with the Apostle of the circumcision. As for his own mission to the Gentiles, James had advocated the broadest extension of Christian immunities, so in return Paul was ready with the utmost concessions to local and to Jewish prepossessions—'the many thousands of believers, all zealots for the law' (A. xxi. 20). On neither side is there need for apologies, only for admiration of Christian breadth and brotherhood. In the particular issue—as in the larger hope which it symbolised—all proved vain: but James must have welcomed with profound relief the news of Paul's safe conduct to Cæsarea, and two years later of the changed venue for trial, and his safe arrival at the Capital.

The accession of Nero in A.D. 54, and the fall of Pallas in 55, bore fruit in the recall of Felix. Josephus deals lightly with his vices, and applauds his severities. Tacitus[1] seems truer to history when he writes 'His ill-timed acts of repression kindled new breaches of the peace,' and dismisses him with the bitter epigram, 'In a career of cruelty and lust he wielded the powers of a despot with the instincts of a slave.' He had sown dragon's teeth, beyond the power of his successor, Porcius Festus, to eradicate. For a brief season[2] the adroit and vigilant opportunism of Festus, helped by the influence of James and the party of order, retarded the catastrophe: but his untimely death in A.D. 62 signalised the

[1] Tac. *Ann.* xii. 54, *Hist.* v. 9.
[2] There is conflict of evidence on the exact date of the supersession of Felix, or of the arrival of Festus; but A.D. 60 seems most probable.

triumph of the extremists. In the three months which elapsed
before the arrival of his successor Albinus, Annas (or Ananus) the
younger, last and most headstrong of the ill-omened Annas stock[1],
assumed the High-priestly power, convened a sitting of the
Sanhedrin[2], usurped the life and death prerogative, and re-
suscitating the fatal precedent—the charge of 'blasphemy'
levelled with deadly effect against Jesus, against Stephen, and
against James the son of Zebedee—executed sentence of stoning
upon 'James, the brother of Jesus and others with him'[3] upon the
very steps of the Temple. "Thus did he bear witness; and they
buried him on the spot beside the temple, and his pillar is there
to this day beside the temple 'True witness he to Jews and
Greeks, that Jesus is the Christ.'[4] And straightway Vespasian
began the siege." The chronological foreshortening is inaccurate;
yet it enforces the true historic sequence. The death of James dates
the final breach between the synagogue and the Church. This is
no mere dictum of Church historians; it is confirmed, even by
Josephus, and finds corroboration in the prolific growth of ec-
clesiastic tradition, invention and romance which sprouted and
clustered round his memory. To pacify the friends of law and
order[5], outraged at this judicial murder, Albinus did indeed

---

[1] θρασὺς τὸν τρόπον καὶ τολμητὴς διαφερόντως is the description in
Jos. *Ant.* xx. ix. 1.

[2] ...καθίζει συνέδριον κριτῶν Jos. *Ant.* xx. ix. 1.

[3] In particular details there are discrepancies, more or less material,
between the accounts of Hegesippus (*ap.* Euseb. *H. E.* ii. 23) and the
brief statement of Josephus *Ant.* xx. ix. 1, but nothing that touches the
main fact of martyrdom. Even the fantastic version of Clem. *Recog.*
1. lxx confirms the outstanding incident. Suspicion was fastened on the
description of James as ἀδελφὸν Ἰησοῦ τοῦ λεγομένου Χριστοῦ, but the best
modern criticism rejects theories of interpolation; nor is the main fact
in any case affected. S.P.C.K. *Biblical Studies* provide a short monograph
on Josephus' references to Jesus by Prof. W. E. Barnes, and Klausner
Jesus of Nazareth pp. 55–60 submits them to careful examination.

[4] These words seem to represent the actual inscription.

[5] The words of Josephus ὅσοι δὲ ἐδόκουν ἐπιεικέστατοι τῶν κατὰ τὴν
πόλιν εἶναι καὶ περὶ τοὺς νόμους ἀκριβεῖς βαρέως ἤνεγκαν ἐπὶ τούτῳ
Ant. xx. ix. 1 must primarily mean Pharisees. *B. J.* ii. xiv. 1 regards
Albinus as a ringleader in organised pillage: to line his own pockets
with wealth, he set imprisoned brigands and malefactors at large, and
handed over Jerusalem to the reprisals of priestly (Sadducean) factions,

require the summary deposition of Annas, but already, with the connivance it would seem if not the actual instigation of Albinus, the boat was in the rapids swirling downwards to the headlong plunge.

and the horrors of mob-rule (*Ant*. xx. ix. 4). His successor Florus (A.D. 64–66) outdid him in bare-faced rapacity. See Fairweather *Background of the Gospels* p. 200.

CHAPTER XII

VALUES OF THE EPISTLE

The Epistle, then, belongs to an era of transition, during which James was the appointed instrument for preserving the connexion between the old dispensation and the new, the Mosaic and the Christian, the Synagogue and the Church. He stands for the continuity of revelation, perhaps the most urgent of all issues for the Jewish Church of the first days. For the existence of Jewish Christianity it was a matter of life and death to reconcile acceptance of Jesus as Lord and Christ with unimpaired faith in Jehovah. To the Jew a breach between the Old Covenant and the New foretold by prophecy[1], a surrender of the Promises, the Law and the Scriptures, was not only an apostasy, but in effect a repudiation of his monotheistic belief in the one Lord God. The Mosaic dispensation was the forecourt of the Christian sanctuary. It is easy to take for granted a settlement which in the end received undisputed assent, and which left few records of controversy in its wake. But the risk of severance was neither slight nor imaginary, and it is easy to see how deeply the issue affected the thought and outlook of Jewish Christianity. It hinged above all upon the acceptance of the Jewish Scriptures: did the acceptance of Jesus confirm or confute, annul or fulfil, the revelation which they enshrined? The solutions offered differ widely, but each was an endeavour to maintain the solidarity of Christianity with the religion out of which it sprang. In the Gospels this is the one theme of constructive teaching attributed to the risen Lord—'Beginning from Moses and from all the prophets, he interpreted to them in all the Scriptures the things which concerned himself' (L. xxiv. 27). That is to say, a true exegesis of the canonical Scriptures pointed to Jesus as their goal. He crowned and completed the purpose of the ages. This is the

---

[1] Jer. xxxi. 31, on which Heb. viii. 13, xii. 24 supply the comment of Judaic Christianity.

climax of the Epistle to the Ephesians: while in the earlier
Epistles of St Paul the sudden and unexpected excursions into
Rabbinic exposition, in the treatment of O.T. texts and types,
are another form of tribute to his sense of the continuity of
revelation. In the Gospel according to Matthew, most closely
associated with Aramaic and Palestinian[1] Christianity, it assumes
the scribal form of the argument from prophecy, based on a
selective marshalling of proof-texts from the Prophets and the
Psalmists. In the Epistle to Hebrews the opening affirmation,
on which the whole conduct of the argument rests, is founded
on the validity of Scripture as the authentic voice and forecast,
which furnishes the credentials and the key to the fuller revelation
in the person of the Son. 'God who in many parts and many
modes hath in old time spoken unto the fathers in the prophets,
hath in these last days spoken unto us in a Son' (Heb. i. 1–2).
That is the bed-rock of Jewish Christianity. Among the ferment
of conflicting religions, cults and systems which fought for recognition in the Orient, Gnosticism in its manifold and tangled
varieties may be used as a convenient label for grouping together
schools of thought which, in more or less distant touch with
Christianity, sought access to the Divine through other modes—
mythologic, ceremonial, mystic or speculative—than those of
self-revelation to a chosen people, or incarnation in a Divine
Son. All alike were in intrinsic conflict with Judaism and with
Jewish Christianity: they may be said to begin with Simon
Magus in Samaria, and to culminate in perhaps the most robust
and effective of second century heresiarchs. Following the tracks
of Tatian, Marcion disowned allegiance to the Old Testament,
and brushing aside all compromise, all subterfuges of development and gradual clarification, maintained that the gulf between
Christianity and Judaism was irreducible. For the new wine the

[1] According to the general view of commentators, though 'Syrian'
may be substituted, if (with Streeter) the Gospel is to be associated with
Antioch. Cf. Wellhausen *Introd.* 62 'Matthew has in view the primitive
Church of Jerusalem, which sought to hold fast by Judaism in spite of
everything.' See Moffatt *Introd. N.T.* p. 256, and Montefiore *Syn.
Gosp.* I. lv.

old wineskins were unserviceable[1]. The attributes of Jahweh, the requirements of the Law, the morality of the Old Testament, belonged to a lower order of religion, the product of an inferior deity or demiurge upon a lower level than God the Father revealed by Jesus Christ the Son. The dualism was as final as that which separated Christianity from Paganism, and spirit from matter.

James exhibits no direct traces of these reactions of Christian thought, which lay as yet beyond his own horizons; for him Rabbinic erudition and corroborative prophecy are too scholastic in method, Alexandrine typology and Gnostic speculation, too wayward and remote; yet they represent tendencies of thought, against which consciously or unconsciously he drew the inner ramparts of defence. The fixed presupposition of his teaching, like that of Jesus himself[2], was the Old Testament, focussed on large lines as a catholic unity, and brought to the touchstone of the authority of Jesus: therein lay the Christian differentia. On verbal exegesis, on ritual and legal and hieratic embellishments he lays no stress; for him what mattered and was vital was comprised in the imperishable summary 'The Lord our God, the Lord, is one; and thou shalt love the Lord thy God with all thy heart and with all thy soul and with all thy mind and with all thy strength....and thou shalt love thy neighbour as thyself.'[3] True to the classic tradition of Jewish prophecy, James was content to rest all upon the ethical appeal. To some this seems second-best, and to denote a lower grade of inspiration than the doctrinal or demonstrative. This underlay the judgment of Luther, when he relegated this Epistle to inferior rank as an Epistle of straw[4]. That was a new criterion of canonicity, which belonged only to a passing phase; and for Luther himself it would have been better

[1] Mk. ii. 22 is the take-off text from which Marcion started his assault.

[2] The entire dependence of Jesus on the O.T. is justly emphasised by Headlam *Life and Teaching* pp. 131, 312, *Jesus Christ in Faith and Teaching* pp. 79 ff., and Temple *Christ's Revelation of God*.

[3] Mk. xii. 29–31, cf. L. x. 27.

[4] In his German Bible this Epistle, in company with the Epistle of Jude, the Epistle to the Hebrews, and Revelation, is relegated to a place at the end. His lead was followed by Coverdale (1535) and Matthew (1537), but finally reversed in *The Great Bible* of 1539.

if he had accorded more commanding weight to the ethical values in religion.

But in such judgments there is an element of truth: the index of ethical values rests not on the bare written word, but also on the conditions and the character from which that word proceeds. Divorced from their context the most moving and memorable of ethical apophthegms ' *Sancta simplicitas*'—'God help me, I can no other'—'Almost at home'—'That shall be the first burned'— or even 'Into thy hands I commend my spirit' and 'It is finished' become but moral commonplaces. There are some to whom the words of James read as mere reflexions or injunctions of the sheltered moralist, without specific context or application; and they rate them accordingly. To myself the accent of conviction, the tension of moral concentration and resolve, run through all; and the circumstances which begat them are the measure of their vitality. More than this—they give the clue to the reserves and the omissions which are a feature of the Epistle, and which the critics are prone to attribute to lack of spiritual receptivity, or to deadened power of response. There is the twofold reticence—to orthodox and ceremonial Judaism on the one hand, and to institutional and doctrinal Christianity on the other. They must be considered separately; and it is a mistake to assume that a common formula or motive will cover both. Silence it is urged implies a lack of realism, or of outspokenness in the writer; or else it is an evidence of late date, and want of fixed objective, when Judaism as a sacrificial or even ceremonial system had already died a natural death, and there was nothing to be gained by raking in the embers. It is an easy explanation, but not available for those who believe in Jacobean authorship. For them defence must run on other lines.

1. Among the outstanding sins against which the writer warns his hearers, none receives more prominence than the temper and the practice of religious controversy. The war-cries of the Herodian Pharisee or Sadducee, the nicer casuistries of Scribal law, the fierce contentions of Shammai and Hillel disputants, were all alike symptoms of the spirit which he strove to exorcise. The process of exposure, whether by denunciation or enforcement,

would equally have been a repudiation of his Christian hope. He was himself a strict and devout conformist, daily frequenting the Temple courts for offices and observances of religion; but these were privileges to be prized, not burdens[1] to be thrust upon the proselyte or the Godfearing. 'The key of knowledge' was not committed to the specialist; the locks set upon the sanctuary were none other than single-hearted faith in God and unfeigned love of man. And in this concentration upon the ethical appeal James is faithful to the precedent set by Jesus himself, throughout the record of his Galilæan ministry. If in personal practice Jesus observed and met enactments of the Law, the hall-mark of his public teaching consists in ethical not institutional requirement. Between the Sermon on the Mount and the Epistle of James, one marked contrast is in the attitude to Pharisaism; and the explanation is not far to seek. The denunciations of Pharisaism recorded in the Gospel are so scathing and emphatic, that we exaggerate the part they played in the actual ministry of Jesus. Most if not all may be referred to certain episodes which took place in Jerusalem[2]; they represent a single aspect of his relation with Pharisees, or rather with that section of the official Pharisees, whose jealous and vindictive bigotry made them at last accomplices in the arrest and trial and crucifixion. But it must not be forgotten that Pharisees were among his hearers and sympathisers, and that even at Jerusalem a Pharisee rescued his dead body from the Cross, and provided place and rites of sepulture. In the years that followed, religious motives were more and more subordinated to political; the supreme moral issue was the peace of Jerusalem, peace within and peace without. On that hope James staked all. Jews of the Dispersion cannot be classified in terms of local groups or schools; and for wider propaganda he perforce depended on the Synagogue. But, at the centre, those to whom James was

[1] Cf. Acts xv. 28 μηδὲν πλέον ἐπιτίθεσθαι βάρος πλὴν τῶν ἐπάναγκες.
[2] So Abrahams *Studies of Pharisaism* I. 13. In any case, the contrast between Mark and Matthew in the measure dealt out to the Pharisees is striking and instructive. Even in the Passion narrative Mark does not once bring a collective charge against the Pharisees, but introduces them only as 'certain of the Pharisees,' or as 'elders,' *sc.* representatives serving on the Sanhedrin.

by tradition and temperament attached, those who were still 'looking for redemption' (L. ii. 38, xxiv. 21), those on whom he built his hopes of a redeemed and liberated Israel, must have belonged chiefly to the following of the Pharisees. Among such, by the magnetism of dauntless conviction and of holy living, he consolidated at Jerusalem a Christian 'brotherhood,'[1] which commanded the respect and the sympathy of sister churches throughout the Dispersion, and when death at last bestowed the martyr's crown, it was they who rescued his dead body from indignities, and called to condign account the author of the crime.

As regards sacrificial and priestly rites, the vital forces of Judaism no longer centred in the Temple and its worship, but in the teaching and devotions of the Synagogue. It is strange how insignificant a place the former occupy in Christian literature; not even enough to date the Gospels by: and no spiritual values are attached to them in the recorded teaching of the Rabbis[2]. At bottom this was the inevitable result of the Exile and the Dispersion. But over and above this, the Temple of Herod had no living root in the sanctities and instincts of the historic faith. The colossal blocks of marble masonry[3], the colonnaded porticoes, the Corinthian capitals, the golden eagle mounted upon the entrance gate, did not—like the ark, or the cherubim, or the Holy of Holies—awaken and enshrine sacred memories; rather they were emblems of the opulence and self-aggrandisement of the Idumæan usurper—material monuments of crumbling decadence. The verdict of history is conclusive. Hardly was the whole complete, when in the final conflagration it was consumed to dust and ashes, and with it the whole order of the Levitical system. The catastrophe extinguished nationality—but on the religious

---

[1] For references, see p. 34 n.

[2] True even of the Epistle to the Hebrews—in some ways the most significant case of all. Of Rabbinic literature, I speak only at second-hand, yet find Edersheim writing: 'We cannot recall a single instance in which these' (sc. the spirit and meaning as opposed to form and letter of these rites) 'were in any proper sense discussed or even referred to in the religious teaching of the Rabbis' *Hist. Jewish Nation* p. 130. And in writers like Montefiore and Abrahams I find the same kind of silence.

[3] Jos. *Ant.* xv. xi, *B. J.* v. iv–v.

unity of Judaism it hardly inflicted a blow[1]. Jamnia and other
schools did but confirm the titles and inaugurate the era of Rabbinic Judaism. In his relations with the Jew, the proselyte, and
the Gentile, St James' one concern was with that organic brotherhood which lay at the heart of religion, not with the framework
or the forms; on them he held his peace, and no word of praise
or of reproof could have done other than contract and weaken
the range of his spiritual appeal. For this reason he religiously
refrains from all reference to the major rites of sacrifice or
circumcision, to the keeping of sabbaths or new moons, to
variant customs that concerned washings or meats—unclean or
strangled—to tabus of social intercourse: in such matters he was
prepared to obey, not to argue; they involved considerations
which would only confuse and complicate the moral issue, and
distract his hearers from the paths of reconciliation, unity and
peace.

2. And to Christianity, as in honour bound, he deals out the
same measure. To institutional or particularist observances—to
baptism or to love-feasts or to Eucharistic celebrations—he makes
no reference; nor again to the exercise of 'spiritual gifts'—tongues,
prophecy or healing[2]. How far they formed part of Church order
and practice among the Christians of Jerusalem it is hard to say:
but the silence of James cannot be construed as decisive. So far
indeed as the evidence goes[3], sacramental observance at Jerusalem
adhered to the simple 'breaking of bread' at the social Agape
or Love-feast, coupled with thankful expectation of the Lord's
return, and with this the note of the Epistle is in full accord.
Sacrificial aspects of the rite were irreconcileable with the con-
tinuance of Temple sacrifice and ritual; but neither topic was
fit matter for an encyclical appeal of this kind to Israel of the
Dispersion.

The same rule applies in the field of Christian doctrine. When

[1] Fairweather *Background of the Gospels* p. 201.
[2] The one illustration which he uses, that of anointing with oil for
healing of the sick (v. 14–15) was at least as familiar to the Synagogue as
to the Church.
[3] See Leitzmann *Messe und Herrenmahl* for a full digest and study of
the materials.

we pass to Christology, the position at Jerusalem goes far to account for the silence respecting the closing incidents in the life of Jesus. For a teacher at Jerusalem seeking to win Jews to acceptance of belief in Jesus as prophet or as Christ, references to the crucifixion were inadmissible. Beyond all else the Cross was to the Jews a 'stumbling-block'; it made acceptance of Jesus as 'the Christ' an affront to the theocracy, a 'blasphemy' against the Law, and high treason to the cause of nationality; to those directly implicated, Sadducees or Pharisees, it was the red rag of infuriation, the imputation of an unpardonable crime. 'Your wish is to bring this man's blood upon us' was the charge brought against Peter and John by the Sanhedrin[1]. On this count silence was the one hope of conciliation. The Resurrection did not stand on the same footing, except in so far as it was a corollary of the crucifixion, and put forward as a vindication of the innocence of Jesus and his acceptability with God: and these were sufficiently expressed in the title of homage and the conviction of his imminent return[2]. But the doctrine of a resurrection was a recognised apple of discord between the contending elements at Jerusalem. The prominence as a dividing line is emphasised by Josephus[3], as well as in the Gospels: and at Jerusalem a mere reference to it by Paul (A. xxiii. 6 ff.) was the signal for a tumultuous outbreak of party strife. In an epistle such as this—addressed not to Christian catechumens, but general, positive and missionary in its appeal—references either to the Crucifixion or to the Resurrection could have no place in the message of one 'preaching the Gospel of peace.' They would have defeated their own aim.

The silence does in truth go far to establish the date and place of composition. No rival hypothesis gives so natural and reasonable an account of omissions, which are at first blush surprising. They confute at once the suggested parallelism with Clement of

---

[1] Acts v. 28, with which compare Gal. iii. 13, v. 11, 1 Cor. i. 23.

[2] So expressly Peter, in his first proclamation of the Resurrection; 'God hath made him both Lord and Christ, this Jesus whom ye crucified' A. ii. 31–6. Even the title 'Christ' had to be used with circumspection at a time when every leader of revolt made it his rallying cry.

[3] Jos. *Ant.* XVIII. i. 4, *B.J.* II. viii. 14.

Rome. His grip on doctrinal theology is in much loose and precarious; but his Christology shows no such suppressions: Jesus Christ 'high priest and guardian of our souls' (lxi, lxiv) is invoked as Saviour (lviii, lix) and Redeemer (xii), who 'for the love he had towards us did give his blood for us by the will of God, his flesh for our flesh, and his soul for our souls' (xlix), and as son and servant receives an equality of dignity with God (xlvi). In this particular, contrast not likeness is the noticeable trait.

In other forms the same is true of the *Didache*; broadly, too, of Justin Martyr and the Apologists; and still more of Alexandrine thought, as exemplified in the Epistle to the Hebrews, or in the Epistle of Barnabas with his interpretation of the letter T as prophetic of the Cross: while as representing Syrian and Asiatic Christianity, Ignatius and Polycarp show the very opposite trend in Christian habits of thought; there is indeed nothing to give countenance to the theory of early Christian apocryphists, for whom the Crucifixion and the Resurrection had dropped into a secondary place of interest or importance, except certain productions of Gnostic aim and colour, which sought to evacuate the Cross and the Resurrection of historic actuality or significance; and with these our Epistle shows no sign of affinity.

But whatever allowance be made for accommodation to circumstances and environment in his presentment of Christianity, we must beware of imputing to the author deliberate suppression of beliefs vital to the Christian profession. The historical interest of the Epistle lies in the evidence which it supplies as to the beliefs regarded as essential in the early church at Jerusalem. In fundamentals James stood upon the ancient ways, the Fear of God, and Faith in God, which were his spiritual birthright. To the devout Jew the *fear* of God meant reverent and scrupulous obedience to the will of God declared and revealed in Holy Writ. 'If ye fear me, keep my commandments,' was his binding rule: and faith in God meant certitude of His existence, resort to Him in prayer, trust in His overruling providence, and an unfaltering assurance of the fulfilment of the promises made to his covenanted people. On this ancestral deposit had supervened the witness and the life of Jesus of Nazareth; a re-interpretation of the oracles and

purposes of God. The teaching of Jesus was no repudiation or revolt
against the old[1]: there is nowhere a precept, hardly even a phrase
or figure, for which some parallel cannot be adduced from Scripture, or from Apocrypha, or from the recorded teaching of contemporary or early Rabbinism. Its originality and momentum
lay rather in selection, in omission, in directness and simplicity,
in proportion of emphasis, in intensity of concentration upon the
soul-relationship with God. It was an emancipation of Judaism
from parasitic growths. And alike in his fidelity to Scripture, and
his ethico-religious concentration, James follows implicitly the
lead of Jesus. Accepting his teaching as the canon of true interpretation, he makes no attempt to innovate, to disintegrate, or to
wrest the words of Scripture to recondite meanings, for party or
doctrinal ends. But under his leadership, the mother-church at
Jerusalem learned to regard the Jewish Scriptures as their spiritual
heritage and the sheet-anchor of their faith, and to take their part
(perhaps decisive for the issue) in incorporating the sacred books
intact in the accepted Canon of the Church of Christ. It was a
momentous contribution to the continuity of revelation and
religion.

The ethic of Jesus has been criticised as a contraction of the
sphere of religion, as a narrowing of human outlook and interests
to a futile and a sterile otherworldliness, as an abandonment
and renunciation of the national mission and aspirations[2]. James
is open to the same reproach, and may be regarded as the first
illustration of the Christian ethic placed *vis-à-vis* with political
and social exigencies. For him, as a true-born Jew, religion was
definitely *a way of life*, a continuous and practical consecration
of behaviour in every action and relationship. Under Pharisaic
and Scribal readings this might and often did degenerate into the

---

[1] At least no overt repudiation, though the principles which he applied
involved its partial abrogation, and its eventual supersession. Torah
and Jesus could not remain in harmony: the two were fundamentally
incompatible, cf. Herford *Pharisaism* p. 143, Robertson *Pharisees and
Jesus* pp. 71, 112, Scott *Ethical Teaching of Jesus* pp. 30–6.

[2] Klausner, after his summary of the Ethic of Jesus, upholds this
thesis, and finds in it the justification of the Jewish rejection of the claims
and Messiahship of Jesus—but Liberal Judaism is vehement in its repudiation of this nationalist creed. Montefiore *O. T. and After* pp. 567–8.

minute prescriptions and disciplines of an external regimen: but following the lead of Jesus[1], James adopted a moral principle as the sovereign arbiter, entitled to prevail over all axioms of tradition or self-interest. He does not belittle or pass judgment upon other factors; but, for the Christian, the primary factor in religion is ethical and altruistic; and, in comparison with that, the rest cease to be of moment. Even in 'observance,' religion 'pure and undefiled' is measured by ethical, not ceremonial or doctrinal or secular obligations. He fastened on the most fixed determinative element in Christian belief, and for good or evil, he committed the Christian community to the ethic of renunciation and of love. In that *milieu* it was the one basis upon which it could remain consistently true to its ideal, and exemplifies the Christian paradox which has so often defied all forecasts of the historian. On that basis it held aloof from fratricidal and from suicidal strife; it grew and multiplied; it enlisted the sympathy and the support of churches near and far; it crystallised into a spiritual brotherhood, which even after its leader's death remained compact and homogeneous enough to secede in a body to Pella, there to take shelter from the cataclysm in which national and institutional Judaism was finally submerged, and from thence to pass on the Gospel torch[2] to daughter sects and churches, which sought to clothe their Christian faith in Eastern garb and forms of thought. That these should diverge widely from the formulas attained by Western Christendom is natural and indeed inevitable: for those are the result of later reflexion, and the impact of wholly different traditions, presuppositions and modes of thought.

[1] See p. 120 n. for references, and cf. Kittel *Religion of the People of Israel* p. 224. 'The O.T. was summed up in him. There was nothing truly great there, which he did not adopt and represent in his own person....He not only pointed the way: He was the way....the One in whom the age was fulfilled.'

[2] Hort *Judaistic Christianity* p. 175: 'The body which migrated to Pella would consist mainly of those who best represented the position formerly taken by St James.' To them many of the best authorities (Zahn, Harnack, Duchesne, etc.) attribute the *Gospel of the Hebrews*, as well as other lost works, once current in Eastern Christendom: and from them some at least of the Syrian churches derived their lineage.

The parting of the ways is seen in James. Regarding the person of Jesus he has no theories to propound. In his teaching he hears the Master's voice and the note of plenary authority: but neither his death, nor his rising again, nor his return to judgment suggests any train of speculative theology. For a logic of forgiveness[1] or atonement Judaism felt no need; it was an attribute of God, part of his prerogative of mercy; on the part of the sinner the one condition of its bestowal was penitence; and in the teaching of John the Baptist and Jesus this had been emphasised in the call to repentance, a change of heart (μετάνοια). God might authorise or approve certain forms of expiation, but no theories were broached to explain their efficacy. And nowhere in the teaching of James is there any suggestion of a mediatorial theory of forgiveness or of any attempt to associate it with the death upon the Cross. Western doctrines of atonement owed much to the forensic and juristic instincts of Rome; these did not affect the East, which turned rather, as in the Epistle to the Hebrews, to the religion of sacrifice; while Temple rites continued, ceremonial and sacrificial expiation possessed but secondary interest for the infant Church, and the affiliations of James throughout are with Pharisaism[2] and the Synagogue.

In the budding Eastern Church the doctrine of Sin and redemption was derived from the theology of Incarnation; but in the first stage of Christianity the idea of Incarnation was remote and alien to the Jewish outlook; it did not and could not enter into the minds of the disciples who 'continued with Jesus in his temptations'; it was the outcome of reflexion upon the Resurrection, upon remembered and recorded utterances, upon new spiritual experiences accorded to the first generation of believers: it formed no part of the Messianic hope or expectation,

[1] On Forgiveness see Edersheim *Life and Times* i. 508. In his First Series of *Studies in Pharisaism* Abrahams devotes two valuable sections (XIX and XX) to Rabbinic Teaching on *God's Forgiveness* and *Man's Forgiveness*, with many references. For a historical survey see Rashdall *Idea of Atonement*.

[2] This is well brought out in Knox *St Paul and the Church of Jerusalem* Chap. I. The points on which James lays chief stress are just those which would most engage the sympathy of the devout Pharisees. His Christianity is conciliatory and eirenic.

R 9

and in no way originated from that source. On this side the out-look of St James hardly goes beyond that of the Synoptic Gospels. But on the ethical side the acceptance of Jesus as *Messiah* involved and effected a profound change of values. Alike for the individual and the nation it turned its back upon ideals of earthly or material ambitions, of spectacular pomp or secular supremacy, of revenge or even recompense for wrongs inflicted, and substituted the ideal of 'the suffering servant.' 'My kingdom is not of this world' was the last word of the Master. For this very reason it was abhorrent to political and patriotic Judaism, in whose eyes Christians became traitors to the cause and spiritual renegades. In personal life, not Torah or Halachah but the authority of Jesus Christ became the arbiter of moral obligation, and his example the criterion of righteousness: and with him lay the final award, '*the crown of life*' (i. 12) promised to them that love him. This meant a revision, even a revolution, in the calculus of virtues. It deposed from the place of pride the traditional and self-regarding virtues of conformity, of propriety, of disciplined and anxious self-respect, and gave the precedence to the altruistic and even self-effacing virtues of endurance, meekness, forgiveness, humility, imposed by the autocracy of love. These, whatever consequences might follow in their train, were the corner-stone on which the new Israel was to be built. It is no wonder that in high places it met with scornful and determined reprobation.

The message of James is in no sense final or complete: his mission was exceptional and temporary[1]. He was not of the apostolic band; he contributes little or nothing to constructive organisation or theology, or to interpretation of the personality of Jesus Christ. He is the minister of transition, leading his people from the land of bondage to the land of promise; he bridges the gulf between Judaism and Christianity, and mediates the passage from the old dispensation to the new. Unfaltering loyalty to the old does not militate against adherence to the new; on the contrary, the Law and the Prophets and the Scripture were

[1] As Hort puts it he was the mouthpiece of 'a temporary duality within Christendom, which from the circumstances of the case was inevitable.' *Judaistic Christianity* p. 83.

to him the authentic voucher for the spiritual kingship of Him who fulfilled their forecasts and satisfied their expectations. Upon this footing he gathered into the Christian garner the ripened yield of Judaism, 'he loosed the middle wall of partition,'[1] and baptised the religious experience of Israel into the Gospel of Jesus Christ. He filled a place impossible for Peter, and much more for a Paul. It was beyond his power to carry with him the nation as a whole, or to avert eventual disruption, but for the new Israel, which he conducted through the wilderness, he not only welded together a Christian brotherhood on a more profound and far-reaching moral ideal centring in personal loyalty to Jesus as the Christ, but he bequeathed to it the imperishable witness of a consecrated and consistent life, crowned and ratified by the heroic death, which sounded the knell of those who instigated and inflicted it.

Historical parallels are always faulty, and if pushed too far misleading, but *mutatis mutandis* James is the Latimer of the Judæo-Christian Reformation. Hugh Latimer was born of homely peasant stock. Son of pious parents, he was schooled to industrious learning, and became devout in his attachment to the traditional forms of faith and worship—'as obstinate a papist as any was in England.' Not till middle life was he won by one destined 'to suffer death for God's word sake,' to closer study of the Scriptures. 'I began to smell the word of God, and forsook the school-doctors and such fooleries.' By stress of circumstances, rather than by any thirst for power or consciousness of administrative gifts, he found himself at the centre of warring forces, religious, political, ecclesiastical. In a diocese torn with religious strife, amid the clash of vested interests, he stood for righteousness, for honest and consistent following of the precepts of Christ. In spite of manifest abuses and perversions, of ecclesiastical prejudice and greed, he clung still to the ancient uses of worship and belief, in faith that the royal law would redeem them from all evil. Muzzled, but not silenced, he raised his voice against the greed of politicians, the worldliness of wealth, the presumption and the pomp of Pharisees. Finally, he died the martyr's death; and at the stake lit 'such a candle, as should never be put out.'

[1] Eph. ii. 14.

Like James, he became the popular hero of the Christian Reformation. His martyrdom, as none other, laid hold upon the imagination of believers, as an ensample of holy living and dying, as a beacon-light of Christian reformation. By force of character not learning, by intrepidity not erudition, he prevailed; and beyond all learning of divines and theologians, his words lived on and wrought in the hearts of the people. To this day his sermons hold a unique place in the roll of 'Every Man's Library.'

Ethics do not cover the whole field of religion or philosophy—but the Christian consciousness was rightly guided, when it finally included in the Canon of the New Testament an Epistle, which—even if not of Apostolic authorship—derived from Christian ethos—pure and simple—its warrant of 'God-given inspiration.'[1]

---

[1] θεόπνευστος (2 Tim. iii. 16).

CHAPTER XIII

EPILOGUE ON THE *CLEMENTINE*
RECOGNITIONS AND *HOMILIES*

No survey of the position and teaching of St James would be complete without some reference to that literature of religious romance which came into being a century and more after his death, but in which so significant a place is given to his memory and his martyrdom. The Eastern colour of the *Clementine Recognitions* and *Homilies*, and their mode of composition, give them a place of their own among the products of apocryphal literature, and they afford strange glimpses into the mentality of the period and the people for whom they were composed. Speculative interest and curiosity are extraordinarily in advance of any glimmerings of inductive inquiry or research. And in dealing with historical personages and incidents, they stand no closer to facts than the various *Acts* of Apostles, which came into vogue in Hellenistic churches of Asia Minor at about the same period. They are generally supposed to have been composed for detached communities or brotherhoods (Essene or other), which lay outside the main currents of church-life in Antioch or Syria, and represent a strange backwater in religious literature, full of luxuriant and teeming growths, but with little influence on subsequent developments. They are cast in the form of theological romance, a new *genre* which came into vogue in the second and third centuries. The main framework, drawn no doubt from plays modelled on this setting—the Roman father, the fugitive wife Mattidia, the twin brothers kidnapped by pirates and sold into slavery—provides good openings for plot. But nothing could be more perfunctory than the actual execution of 'the recognitions,' by which the younger son Clement, a follower in the train of Peter, identifies and reunites the scattered members of his family. The scene is laid among the Syrian coast towns from Cæsarea and Tyre to Antioch, in which the conflicts of religious cults and philosophies must have been full of stir and interest. But in these pages delineation is feeble and confused; there is little or no topical variety or realism; the outlines of contemporary life and manners are diffuse and blurred; there is no live presentment of heathen cults, or schools of philosophy; no firm grip of current controversies. Place after place becomes a pulpit for tedious disquisitions, in which Peter engages, or is preparing to engage, in wordy debate with his antagonist, Simon Magus, heretic and thaumaturgist. The range of subjects touched or treated is immense, and shows the kaleidoscopic confusion of ideas which resulted from the conflict of religions. There are constant allusions to angelology, demons, and all forms of idolatry, superstitions orgiastic and licentious. In fundamentals, prime stress is laid on the *Monarchia* of the one God, as the author and upholder of all being; polytheism is denounced as immoral and irrational; and heathen gods cannot be regarded as derivative agents of God, though as angels and demons good and evil spirits are ubiquitously active. When the process of creation comes under discussion, conflicting theories are advanced to account for the existence of evil and the Evil One, of sin and suffering in the constitution of things and the being of man. At times the theory of a secondary Creator, a Demiurge of the material universe, seems favourably entertained, and the moral difficulties of the Old Testament, its inner discrepancies and contradictions, its seeming recognition of false gods, the supersession of the Jewish Law and rites, are handled upon Marcionic lines. At other times strange gnostic and theosophic speculations crop up in unexpected places, such for instance as the doctrine of Creation in *syzygies* or pairs of opposites —the two kingdoms, finite and infinite, begotten and unbegotten, Male and Female elements in worship, in religion and in psychology. Zoroaster and Plato, Stoics, Epicureans, Sceptics and Platonists are all laid under contribution, but are seldom used with conviction, or carried to firm conclusion. There is much of the elastic vagueness of modern theosophy. But throughout an order of Providence, and of man's Free Will, is resolutely opposed to doctrines of Determinism[1] and over-ruling Natural

Determinism is called γένεσις, the law of natural evolution—discussed at full length in *Hom.* xiv. and *Rec.* viii.

law (γένεσις). In this strange medley of heterogeneous and heterodox speculations, it is easy to discriminate Ebionite, Marcionite, Gnostic and other strands of teaching, but much harder to reconstitute any society or societies, to which such disquisitions would be acceptable. I conceive of them as religious brotherhoods, somewhat of the Essene type, organised on a community or synagogic basis, and adapting Judaistic Christianity to the moulds of Eastern speculation and forms of Mystery worship. Their doctrines were eclectic and esoteric. The prefatory letter of Peter to James, §§ 3–5, requires of every teacher a probation of six years, and a solemn oath of secrecy respecting the instruction of catechumens. Baptism—the *sine qua non* of salvation[1]—is treated as an initiatory rite, exorcising the demon taint contracted by participation in idol feasts or sacrifice, administered with the trine invocation, and qualifying for admission to the common meal[2]; it was preceded by fasting[3], and associated with running water, or ablutions in the sea[4], linked by natural magic with the mystic properties of water as the germinal and productive principle of life[5]. It was instituted by Christ as a substitute for the religion of propitiatory sacrifice[6]. Eucharistic observance, sometimes under forms of bread and salt[7], but without mention of wine, is resolved into participation in the common meal of the adepts[8], and nowhere is there any teaching of deeper sacramental communion: the atmosphere is that of Ebionite offices, or Mystery cults.

The Christology remains throughout invertebrate, with hardly an attempt at dogmatic definition. The trine invocation at Baptism is accepted and enforced[9], and so too the descriptive designation Son of God, but explicitly as not implying, indeed as excluding, equality with God[10]. Christ—regarded as a parallel to titles of pre-eminence such as Pharaoh, Arsaces, Cæsar, etc.—is explained as 'the man anointed with oil taken from the wood of the tree

---

[1] *Hom.* xi. 25–6, xiii. 21.
[2] *Rec.* i. 19, 69.   [3] *Rec.* vii. 34, 36, 37.
[4] *Rec.* vi. 15, vii. 38, *Hom.* xi. 35, xiv. 1.
[5] *Rec.* vi. 8, viii. 26–7, ix. 7.
[6] *Rec.* i. 37–9, *Hom.* vii. 8.   [7] *Hom.* xiv. 1, *Ep. Peter* § 4.
[8] e.g. *Rec.* vi. 15, vii. 36. *Ep. Clem.* § 9.
[9] *Rec.* i. 69.   [10] *Rec.* i. 45, x. 47; *Hom.* xvi. 15–17.

of life.'[1] The habitual term is 'the true Prophet,'[2] the successor of Adam and Moses, who superseded the Mosaic dispensation—ceremonial and ethical—by the higher revelations of truths which he was commissioned to convey to the chosen people, Gentile[3] as well as Jew. There are no doctrines of Grace, no scheme of redemption or atonement through the Cross: all reference to the Resurrection or Ascension is wilfully avoided, and there is no suggestion of any spiritual union of the believer with Christ. Pauline or Johannine theology might never have existed; and the Epistles of Paul are studiously ignored[4]. In pages that bristle with citations from the Synoptists, and in which the Syrophœnician woman and her daughter, Zacchæus, Gamaliel and the centurion Cornelius, figure as *dramatis personæ*, such omissions tell their own tale.

The Ethic, based on the requirements of Judaism, as revised and sublimated by Christ, loses reality and tends to fall out of touch with life. Participation in all idol feasts or practices is violently denounced; resort to heathen law-courts is prohibited, and social morality is based on nuptial chastity[5]; but delineations of domestic or social habits, occupations and relationships are exasperatingly vague, and are swamped under tedious tirades upon philosophic polemics, astrological[6] figments, heathen rites and immoral myths[7]. The same applies to the handling of Institutional religion. There is much talk of Bishops, with occasional mention of Presbyters, Deacons, Catechists and Catechumens; but their energies expend themselves on homilies and discussions to local groups of believers or disbelievers, to whom the ministry of preaching affords the one channel of grace. Even in the Letter of Clement prefixed to the *Homilies* (§ 2. 3. 20) the 'Chair' of James or Peter is 'the Chair of discourse,'[8] absorbed in continuous instruction and debate. Bishops are

---

[1] *Rec.* i. 45.
[2] *Rec.* i. 16–18, 39–44, ii. 22, v. 10–13 and *passim*; *Hom.* ii. 5–6, iii. 15, 20, 47–53, viii. 6–7.
[3] *Hom.* iii. 19, viii. 6–7.
[4] The one or two apparent exceptions are I think derivative.
[5] *Rec.* vi. 12; *Hom.* xiii. 13–21; *Ep. Clem.* § 7.
[6] *Rec.* ix. 12–24, x. 11–12.   [7] *Rec.* x. 17–39, *Hom.* vi.
[8] τὴν τῶν λόγων καθέδραν.

multiplied as mouthpieces of local congregations, charged with itinerant and controversial propaganda[1]. But any idea of an organic or collective Christendom seems as remote as that of a catholic Creed.

These brackish and stagnant waters may seem hardly worth exploration. Yet their phosphorescent gleams and exhalations belong to the environment, and even in decomposition show the vagaries and the habitudes of thought, among which Judaic Christianity had to struggle for existence. In a world of ideas and contacts so profuse and many-sided it would be hard to find thought more captious and undisciplined, or more barren of result or aim. It circles round, without clear objective, till it becomes a mere eddy of words. With their challenges, encounters, flights, and fantastic metamorphoses, the leading disputants, Peter and Simon Magus, are reduced to travesties of theological debate. With whatever grains of biographical incident and value, Simon may fairly be regarded as a dramatic embodiment, a kind of amalgam or synthesis of Gnostic speculations. But it is harder to excuse the distortions of Peter, whose flights become hardly less esoteric and rambling than those of Simon himself: and the lack of historic realism or perspective is bewildering. Yet throughout they are symptomatic: the religious sense—curiously capricious in taste and choice of traits—reaches out tentacles to the figure of the holy man, yet seems to respond but feebly to the human attractiveness of Jesus. Coupled with indifference to historic fact and actuality, or to any reasoned and consistent scheme of truth, they forecast the destinies of Christianity as the religion of the West, rather than of the Eastern lands from which it sprang. Vital assimilation of the Christian ethic of Jesus built upon the understanding and interpretation of his person, which Hellenic thought alone proved able to attain. For our present purpose there is nothing to be gained by more minute examination of the Prefatory letters fathered upon Peter and his successor Clement—which at a later day furnished the base for the False Decretals. Apart from the express statement of Rufinus[2], that they were later appendages, there is no clue to

---

[1] e.g. *Rec.* iii. 66.

[2] In his Preface to *Clem. Recog.*

precise date or authorship; but their obvious intention is to exalt
the local prestige of Eastern Christendom, and to affirm the
primacy of Jerusalem against the competing pretensions of the
Western Church and Rome. And the laudatory salutations
addressed to James as 'brother of the Lord,' and as 'bishop of
bishops, administering the holy church of the Hebrews at Jerusalem and the churches duly founded everywhere by the providence
of God' subserve this end. But with the main body of the work
the case is different. There, amongst the masqueraders, there
stands one figure in the background impressive and remote, who
never treads the boards, but is referred to as the ultimate fount of
authority and reverence[1]. Ordained bishop[2] in Jerusalem by the
Lord, James there receives reports from the Apostles[3], and com-
municates them to the congregation of believers: one scene is
recounted at length. At the end of the long discourse of Gamaliel,
in answer to the high priest Caiaphas, James undertakes from the
books of the Law and the prophets to prove that Jesus is the
Christ, and that prophecy foretold a twofold Coming, the one
in humiliation already accomplished in his person, the other in
glory and majesty which yet awaits accomplishment. For seven[4]
successive days he enlarged upon this theme, urging upon his
hearers, people and High-priest, the acceptance of Christian
baptism; indignation at his success finally prompted a Temple
fanatic[5] to raise a tumult, in which James was flung headlong
down the Temple steps and left for dead; his faithful followers
were permitted to carry home the body, and under their care
he revived. Thereafter he commissioned Peter 'to teach the word

---

[1] Without wading through the tedious divagations of the *Homilies*
and *Recognitions*, it is not easy to realise the part assigned to James. He
is like the ideal buccaneer of the *Treasure Island*, the Captain Flint, who
never appears and takes no part in the action, but is the good or evil
genius of those who made him their exemplar.
[2] In *Rec.* i. 43 the term may be descriptive, but is certainly titular
in *Rec.* i. 70, 72. In i. 68 and 73 he is styled archi-episcopus.
[3] *Rec.* i. 44.
[4] The 'seven' has probably symbolic value. Cf. *Rec.* i. 43.
[5] In *Rec.* i. 70, a marginal note calls him Saul, borrowing from the
martyrdom of Stephen, and in i. 71 he is sent on to Damascus to make
havoc of the faithful!

of truth' in Cæsarea, to foil the machinations of Simon the wandering heresiarch, and to report progress at regular intervals[1]: from Rome he received full and confidential reports of his acts and declarations[2], and later Clement[3], as successor to Peter, submits formal account of his appointment and installation in the See, with full transcripts of the Apostle's teachings and discourses[4].

The anachronisms and distortions of time and place and sequences of events are absurd; but there remains the indelible impression of a commanding and revered personality, whose moral elevation and insight became to all within his range a standard of that which was sound in belief and practice and avowal[5]. All fit and faithful teachers, it is said, must draw their credentials[6] from James, the brother of the Lord. While the *Homilies* show no verbal acquaintance[7] with the Epistle, the teaching attributed to him bears close and noticeable resemblances. The points singled out are the validity of Old Testament Scriptures —the law and the prophets—as the final court of appeal[8], the proof from prophecy that Jesus is the Christ, the first Coming in humiliation and the promise of his return, 'when he shall give the kingdom to those who believe in him and who observe all things which he has commanded.' In Christian outlook the Ebionite communities, for whom these scriptures were composed, may be said to represent a stunted and perverted growth from the Judaic Christianity of James[9]. Boasting a stubborn adherence to his presentation of the faith, they set their faces against all Pauline or Johannine or Western developments of Christian doctrine, allied their Judaism with a syncretic hash of the philosophic ideas, the gnostic and theosophic fancies, and the ceremonial usages and cults, which they found current among the Hellenised populations of Syro-Phœnicia. On the one hand they are an object lesson in the fantastic caprices and absurdities of

---

[1] *Rec.* i. 71–3.   [2] *Ep. Peter* 1–3.   [3] *Ep. Clem.*
[4] *Rec.* iii. 74–5.   [5] *Hom.* xi. 35   [6] *Rec.* iv. 35.
[7] The correspondences registered by Mayor p. lxvi are quite unconvincing.
[8] *Rec.* i. 68.
[9] The Epistle itself shows no trace of Ebionite influence or peculiarities.

practice and belief, into which the Christian synagogues might have fallen, had not James founded them on the bedrock of ethical conviction and consistency, and knit up the acceptance of Jesus as Lord and Christ with the historic revelation of God in the Jewish scripture and in the person of Jesus. And on the other, by a happy chance, they set their seal to the abiding spiritual ascendancy, which in Eastern churches was associated with the name and leadership of St James.

INDEX

Abraham 40
ἀδελφοί 21, 34, 52, 58
Agrippina 112
ἀκαταστασία 45
Albinus 24, 116
Tib. Alexander 112
Alexandrine Teaching 120
Ananias 112, 113
Ananus 116-17
Annas family 53, 111, 116
Anointing 56, 101, 124
ἀνυπόκριτος 85
Aramaic 36, 39-40

Baptism 30, 135
Barnabas, Epist. 101, 102, 105, 126
Bishop 29, 136
'Blanched' theology 83, 108
Breaking of Bread 26, 30
Brigandage 31, 111
Brotherhood, Christian (see ἀδελφοί) 124, 128, 131

Caligula 111
Christians, at Jerusalem 25-9, 110-16, 128
  Name 89
  Numbers 29
Christology 65-6, 88-95, 108, 125, 126, 129-30, 135
Christs, 'false' 43, 49, 112, 125
Claudius 111, 112
Clement Alex. 28, 98
Clement of Rome 83, 88, 102, 104-5, 108, 125-6
Clementine Homilies and Recognitions 29, 54, 133-40
Collections for Jerusalem 58, 113
Confession 56
Contentiousness 49, 50-2, 56, 121
Continuity (of Revelation) 118-19, 127
Covetousness 53, 114

Crucifixion 28, 88, 93, 122, 125, 129
Cumanus 42, 112

Demons 75, δαιμονιώδης 49-50
Determinism 62
Diaspora 11-15, 26-7, 106-7
Didache 83, 88, 102, 105, 126
δίκαιος 93
δικαιοῦσθαι 77
Diognetus, Epist. ad 83, 105
δίψυχος 35, 44, 57, 102
δοκίμιον 44, 84, 96
δόξα 13, 36, 90-2, 97, 99
δωδεκάφυλον 13

Ebionites 104, 139
Elders 56
Endurance 26, 36, 43, 46, 56, 114
Essenes 54, 62, 104, 135
Ethical values 121, 122
Eucharist 30, 135

Factions 28, 48-9, 56, 105, 114, 121
C. Fadus 49, 112
Faith 43, 71-83, 81, 126
Falkland 51
The Fall 66
A. Felix 42, 112, 113, 115
P. Festus 42, 115
Florus 117
Forgiveness (Atonement) 129

Galilee 17, 49
  Culture 39
  Sea of 38
Gamaliel 22, 27
Genesis 65
Gentile vices 45
Glory, see δόξα
Gnosticism 119, 120, 126, 134, 135, 137
Greek language, use of 38-40

Hebrews, Epistle 43, 76, 100, 101, 119
  Gospel of 18
Hegesippus 21 *n.*, 116
Hellenism 27, 39
Hermas 88, 105, 108
Herod 123
  Agrippa I 27, 42, 111
  Agrippa II 111
  Antipas 16–17, 111
Higher Criticism 1–2, 104–5
Hillel 22, 41, 74, 121
Humility 47

Imperatives 34, 98
Institutional Religion 56, 121, 122, 123, 124
Isaiah 40, 53, 97

James, Brother of the Lord 11, 16
  Apostle 12
  Appearance and Person 28
  Asceticism 21, 28, 55
  'Bishop' of Jerusalem 12, 29, 138
  Conservatism 18, 21, 78, 130
  Death 16, 24, 27, 101, 116, 123, 138
  Early life and career 16, 18
  Ethic 20–1, 42–59
  Ethical values 120–2, 127–8
  at Jerusalem—Leadership 12, 19, 20, 28–30, 42, 98, 110–16
  'The Just' 21, 41; Personal holiness 21–2, 55, 57, 126, 138–40
  Opportunism 20, 43, 126
  Pauline contacts 18–20, 78–83, 103, 109, 115
  Pharisees 22–4, 122–3
  Realist 45, 56–8
James, Epistle of:
  Aramaic 36, 104
  Authentic 33
  Canonicity 12, 100, 129
  Date, late 104
  Diction and vocabulary 35, 37
  Ethical 42–59, 66–7, 70, 76, 78, 114, 120, 122, 130

James, Epistle of:
  Form 33
  Grammar, etc. 40
  Greek original 36
  Hebraic background and cast 35, 37, 38, 41, 43, 57
  Hellenism 37, 40
  Jesus' teaching 51, 57, 78, 127, 130
  Law 40, 66–70, 80
  Literary type and affinities 32–3, 34, 35, 38
  Metaphor 37
  Omissions and reserves 50, 57, 66–7, 79, 82–3, 88–9, 121, 124, 125–6
  Pauline relations 78–83
  Prophetic element 40
  Quotation 35
  Scriptures, dependence on 20–1, 40, 104, 105, 118, 120, 127, 130–1, 139
  Septuagint influence 35, 37–9
  Style 34–5, 37, 40
  Topical 30–1, 37–8
  Transitional 118, 130–1
  Wisdom Books 40–1, 50–1
James, son of Alphæus 11
James, father of Judas 11
James, the Little 11
James, son of Zebedee 11, 27
Jerusalem, Council 19–20, 112
  Economic, political and social 31, 43, 110–14
  Mother-Church 28–9, 58
Jesus, Ethical teaching 101, 122, 127, 128, 130
Jewish Christians, at Jerusalem 21, 25, 29, 118, 119, 126, 130
Job 41, 44
Joseph of Arimathæa 22
Josephus 29, 39, 49, 53, 61–2, 112, 115–16
Judaism 57, 78, 82, 101, 120–30, 134
Judas of Galilee 49, 112
Jude 12, 39
Justin Martyr 126

κλύδων 38 n.
Kurios 13, 89–90, 94

Landholders 31–2
Latimer 32, 131
Law 1, 40, 52, 66–70, 74, 80, 82
Liberty 67–8
Literature, Jewish 39–40
Long-suffering 46–55
Luther 120

Marcion 119
Mark, Gospel 101–2
Matthew, Gospel 67–8, 101–2, 119
Messianic Expectation 129–30
μετάγειν 38

Nationalism 27, 130
Neo-Platonic 59–60, 104
Nero 115
Numbers, in Josephus 17, 29

Oaths 54, 67, 102, 104
Old Testament Scriptures 37, 40–1, 53

Pacifism 24, 42, 46, 51, 55, 92, 94–5, 115
Palestine 16–18, 31
Palestinian Christianity 54, 56
    Colouring 31–2, 37
    Dialect 38
παράγειν 38
Parousia 46, 89, 92, 100
Patience, see Endurance, ὑπομονή
Paul and Jerusalem 19–20, 112, 113, 115, 131
    Doctrine 109, 119
    Ethic 42, 45
    Faith and Works 78–83
Peasants 31–2
πειρασμός 36, 44
Pella 128
Persecution 45–6, 100, 105
Peter 27–8, 42, 98, 131, 134–7
    First Epistle 32, 46, 47, 96–100, 107, 109
Pharisaism 61–4, 122, 129

Pharisees 23–4, 49, 111, 116, 121, 122–3, 125
Philip the Tetrarch 17, 111
Pilate (Pontius) 111
πλοῖα 38 n.
Plutocracy 31, 53
Poverty 58, 113
Prayer 55
Prophets 40, 53, 54
προσωπολημψία 36, 75, 84, 97
Proverbs 47

Quadratus, Ummidius 112

Rabbinic schools 124
Rabbinic teaching 74, 119, 120, 123, 127
Rahab 75, 76, 79, 83
Readers 21, 25–33, 58
Resurrection 18, 88, 99, 125
Risings 49
Ritual and Observance 120, 121, 124, 128, 134–5
Roman Rule 42–3
Ep. Romans 84–7, 107 (see Index of Texts)

Sacraments 30, 56, 124, 135
Sadducees 53, 62, 111, 121, 125
Salutation 11–15, 29, 105–6
Scripture 20–1, 40, 104, 105, 118, 119
Sects and Sectarianism 49, 56, 114
Septuagint 37, 39, 40
Sermon on Mount 67, 68, 69, 102, 122
Shammai 22, 74, 121
Shekinah 90–2, 100
Sicarii 43, 114
Sin, Doctrine of 62–6, 129
Sirach 40, 55, 62
Spitta 66
στέφανος 40
Stephen 27
Stoicism 61
Sub-Apostolic writings 102, 104
Synagogue 23, 26, 30, 31, 66, 122–3

Temple 123
Temptation 36, 44, 62–4
θάλασσα 38
Theudas 49, 112
Tiberius 111
Tongue, Sins of 47–8, 52, 55, 114
Traders 32
Tribes, Twelve 13

ὑπομονή 36, 43, 100

Wars 30–1, 49, 51–2, 112
Wealth 46, 53, 93, 114
Widows and Orphans 59
Will, Free Will 62–3
Wisdom 115
   Books and literature 37, 40–1, 50–1
Worldliness 53

Zealots (ζηλοῦν) 43, 111, 114

INDEX OF N.T. TEXTS

Matthew

v, 33–7	67
v, 41, 42	89
v, 48	44
vii, 7	55
viii, 1	18
ix, 2–5	56
ix, 22	72
ix, 29	72
xi, 18	49
xix, 2	18
xxi, 21	55, 72
xxii, 39	35
xxiii	24
xxiii, 2–3	50
xxiv, 24	49
xxiv, 33	58

Mark

i, 31	73
ii, 1–12	56
ii, 22	120
iii, 7–9	18
iii, 21, 31	18
iv, 40	72
v, 9	51
v, 22	26
v, 34–8	26, 54, 72
vi, 13	56, 101
xi, 22	72
xi, 23	55
xii, 29–31	52, 120
xiii, 22	49

Luke

vii, 33	49
vii, 50	72
viii, 15	43
viii, 19	18
viii, 48	72
viii, 41, 49	26
x, 27	120
x, 34	56

Luke

xi, 9	55
xi, 34	57
xiv, 11	47
xvii, 6	72
xvii, 19	72
xxi, 19	43, 44
xxiv, 21	123
xxiv, 27	118

John

i, 14	91
v, 14	56
vii, 3–9	18
vii, 20	50
ix, 2	56
xvi, 4	55

Acts

i, 13–14	18
ii, 36	90, 125
ii, 44–5	58
ii, 46, 47	25
iii, 1, 11	25
iii, 14	93
iv, 34–7	58
v, 1	59
v, 12	25
v, 28	125
v, 39	23
v, 41	89
v, 42	25, 89
vi, 1	59
vi, 9	26
viii, 1, 4	15
viii, 8, 17	26
ix, 1	23
xi, 26	89
xi, 29–30	113
xii, 1, 2	11
xiii, 46	110
xv, 2–4	19
xv, 13	19
xv, 20, 29	20

Acts

xv, 23	14
xv, 28	122
xviii, 18	20
xx, 4	113
xx, 23	115
xxi, 18	20
xxi, 20	23, 115
xxi, 24–6	20
xxii, 14	93
xxii, 17	25
xxiii–xxiv, 3	112
xxiv, 5, 14	25
xxiv, 10 ff.	113
xxvi, 7	13
xxvi, 28	89

Romans

i, 17	79
i, 28–32	45
i, 29	48
ii, 1, 3, 5	85
ii, 4	46
ii, 6, 7	81
ii, 11, 13	80, 84, 86
ii, 12, 25, 27	80, 85, 86
iii, 5, 9	77
iii, 13	48
iii, 21	79
iii, 22	75, 77
iii, 27–28	82
iv, 2, 6	82
v, 4	84
vii, 23	86
viii, 7	86
ix, 4	91
ix, 22	46
x, 3	86
x, 4	68
xi, 18	86
xii, 9	85
xiii, 8, 10	69, 80, 86
xiv, 4	85

1 Corinthians

i, 23	125
ii, 8	36
iv, 21	85
xiii, 12	65

2 Corinthians

ii, 10, iii, 18, iv, 6	65
vi, 6, x, 1	85
ix, 8	81
xii, 15	57

Galatians

i, 3	90
i, 14	78
i, 18–19	19
ii, 9–12	19
ii, 10	20
ii, 12	19
ii, 16	75, 82
ii, 20	75
iii, 2, 5, 10	75, 82
iii, 6	77
iii, 13	125
v, 6	81
v, 11	125
v, 19–20	45
vi, 1	85

Ephesians

ii, 10	81
ii, 14	131
iv, 2	85
iv, 25, 31	48
v, 4	48
vi, 9	85

Philippians

ii, 3, 8, iv, 5	85
iii, 9	75

Colossians

i, 10	81
i, 11	46
iii, 2, 25	85

1 Thessalonians

i, 1	90
ii, 19	40

2 Thessalonians

ii, 17	81

1 Timothy

i, 11	91
vi, 18	81

2 Timothy

iii, 16	132
iv, 8	40
iv, 18	90

Titus

i, 12	75
ii, 7, 14	81
ii, 13	91
iii, 8	81

Hebrews

i, 1–3	91, 100, 119
iii, 7, 13	100
vi, 1, 12	100
viii, 13	101, 118
ix, 5	91
ix, 14	100
x, 25	46, 100
x, 32–4, 36	100
x, 37–9	71
xi	100
xi, 13	15
xii, 1, 3, 7	100
xii, 11	51
xii, 24	118
xiii, 3	100

James

i, 1	11–15, 30, 36, 57, 89
i, 2	46, 62, 96, 98
i, 3	73
i, 3–4	36, 43, 44, 63, 84, 100
i, 5	41, 55
i, 6	38, 55, 73
i, 8	44, 45, 57
i, 9–10	47, 85, 97
i, 11	37, 40, 93
i, 12	36, 40, 57, 58, 97, 100, 130
i, 13–18	63–4
i, 16	58, 86

James

i, 17	64, 86
i, 19	35, 64
i, 20	86
i, 21	34, 97
i, 22	84
i, 23	65
i, 24	93
i, 25	40, 67, 70, 84, 96
i, 26	48
i, 27	59, 96, 128
ii, 1	36, 57–8, 75, 89
ii, 2–6	46, 66
ii, 2	23, 26, 30, 45
ii, 5	34, 67
ii, 6	45
ii, 7	58, 89
ii, 8–11	86
ii, 8	40, 67, 68, 69, 80
ii, 9	75
ii, 10–13	40
ii, 10	69, 75
ii, 11	85
ii, 12	67, 70, 85
ii, 13	35, 86
ii, 14	75, 84
ii, 16	75
ii, 17–26	76, 100
ii, 18	34, 70, 76
ii, 19	50, 75
ii, 20	70, 85
ii, 21–5	40, 75, 77
ii, 22	75
ii, 23	76, 77
ii, 26	35, 76
iii, 1	48, 50, 69
iii, 4	34, 38, 45
iii, 6–8	47, 59–60, 104
iii, 8–9	47, 49
iii, 9–10	68
iii, 12	37, 38, 51
iii, 13	41, 49, 51, 85
iii, 14	48, 114
iii, 15	49
iii, 16	45, 48, 114
iii, 17	41, 50–1, 55, 85, 97
iii, 18	37, 42, 51, 81, 114–15

James		
iii, 21, 25	86
iv, 1	30, 45, 52, 97, 113
iv, 2	55, 113
iv, 3	55
iv, 4	54
iv, 6	37, 47, 85, 94, 97
iv, 7	94, 97, 98
iv, 8	34, 44, 47
iv, 10	34, 47, 85, 97
iv, 11	48, 52, 55, 69, 84, 85
iv, 12	52
iv, 13	34
iv, 13–14	32
iv, 13–16	46, 55
iv, 16	48, 102
v, 1–6	40, 46, 53, 55, 114
v, 1	34, 45
v, 2	37
v, 3	85
v, 4	31, 59, 94, 114
v, 5	30, 37, 55, 85
v, 6	45, 46, 53, 93
v, 7	34, 37, 46, 52, 89, 92

James

v, 7–11	55, 58
v, 8	34, 46, 89, 92
v, 9	52
v, 10	46
v, 11	41, 44, 100
v, 12	52, 54, 67, 102
v, 13–16	46, 55, 66, 93–4
v, 14	56, 101, 124
v, 15	73
v, 16	55, 93, 94
v, 20	40, 97

1 Peter

i, 1	99
i, 3, 6	90, 96
i, 3 ff.	98, 99
i, 11	100
i, 12	96
i, 17	97
i, 19	96, 100
i, 22, 24	85, 97
ii, 1, 11	97
ii, 9, 21, 25	99

1 Peter

iii, 15	99
iii, 18, 22	93, 100
iv, 7, 13	46
iv, 8, 10	97
iv, 13, 14, 18	91, 99, 100
iv, 16	89
v, 1	99, 100
v, 4	41, 97, 99
v, 5	47, 94, 97
v, 6, 8, 9	97

2 Peter

i, 17	92

1 John

ii, 1	93

Jude 1	12
,, 4, 17, 21	90

Revelation

ii, 10	41
v, 13	90
vii, 4–8	14
vii, 12	90

For EU product safety concerns, contact us at Calle de José Abascal, 56–1°,
28003 Madrid, Spain or eugpsr@cambridge.org.

www.ingramcontent.com/pod-product-compliance
Ingram Content Group UK Ltd.
Pitfield, Milton Keynes, MK11 3LW, UK
UKHW012332130625
459647UK00009B/239